Grieving with Mary

Finding Comfort and Healing
in Devotion to the Mother of God

Mary K. Doyle

PUBLICATIONS

Edited by L.C. Fiore
Cover design by Tom A. Wright
Text design and typesetting by Desktop Edit Shop, Inc.
Photos by Mary K. Doyle

Scripture quotes are from the *New Revised Standard Version of the Bible*, copyright ©1989 by the Division of Christian Education of the National Council of the Churches of Christ in the USA. All rights reserved. Used with permission.

Copyright ©2009 by Mary K. Doyle

Published by ACTA Publications, 5559 W. Howard Street, Skokie, IL 60077, (800) 397-2282, www.actapublications.com.

All rights reserved. No part of this book may be used or reproduced in any manner without written permission of the publisher, except in the case of brief quotations embodied in critical articles and reviews. Permission is hereby given to use short excerpts with proper citation in reviews and marketing copy, church bulletins and handouts, and scholarly papers.

Library of Congress Number: 2009925186
ISBN: 978-0-87946-397-7
Printed in the United States of America by Total Printing Systems
Year 17 16 15 14 13 12 11 10 09
Printing 10 09 08 07 06 05 04 03 02 First Edition

Text printed on 30% post-consumer recycled paper.

Contents

Disclaimer

Prayer can offer a sense of calm in difficult times. However, the practice of finding peace and answers through prayer is not being promoted in this book as a replacement for medical care. Although medical miracles are known to occur, prayer is most effective in healing when it is in addition to modern and alternative medicine.

Dedication

I dedicate this book to my aunt, Pauline McCarthy. Aunt Paula offers an unshakeable model of how to grieve with Mary. She puts her troubles in Mary's hands and continues to acknowledge the little joys in life despite enduring some of the world's greatest heartaches.

I pray that our Blessed Mother holds my aunt, my friends and family, and all those who grieve close to her Immaculate Heart, tightly within the warmth and security of her mantle.

Introduction

Holy Rosary Church.
Paia, Maui, Hawaii.

Say Three Hail Marys and Call Her in the Morning

The memory of the day my father died is as clear as if it happened only yesterday. I was enjoying the lovely July sunshine and fresh morning breeze streaming through the windows when Dad's nurse called to tell me he had passed away. The news shouldn't have surprised me. Dad had small-cell carcinoma of the lungs that metastasized to the brain and likely spread throughout his body. I knew the prognosis was not good, and yet the announcement of his death left me stunned.

Immediately after talking with the nurse, I prayed three Hail Marys and began calling family members. There was little time to sort through my thoughts and feelings. The business of death consumed my time. I needed to meet with my brothers and sisters and plan a wake. There were people to notify, bills to pay, and household items to sort.

In the following months, my family did its best to help one another through the grieving process. We told stories about our dad and hugged one another often. We prayed together and individually. I've always had a devotion to Mary, so many of my prayers went to her. In my sorrow, I needed to remain close to my heavenly mother.

ℋ ℋ

Three Hail Marys

Sick, frightened or sad? Say three Hail Marys and ask the mother of Jesus for help. Both my parents and my first teachers, the Sisters of Charity of the Blessed Virgin Mary (BVM), prescribed this remedy to me when I was a child. I have carried on the practice of praying these prayers as one of my first responses to a crisis ever since.

Throughout the many trials, heartaches and anxieties of my life, I prayed, and continue to pray, those three Hail Marys. The practice gives me comfort and a brief period of calm like the eye of a storm. I literally feel the relief, and also the tenderness, of our holy mother. I then am able to think and evaluate the situation more clearly. Most reassuringly, I am reminded that I am never alone—a devoted friend is at my side. Mary will watch over and help me.

The Hail Mary is the prayer of choice because it is the most common and the most loved Marian prayer. People have prayed it in its present form since at least the sixteenth century, and they read segments of it for centuries prior to that. Today the Hail Mary is prayed by itself; repeated three times, often for the intentions of faith, hope and love; or grouped with other prayers, such as when praying the rosary or a novena.

Praying the Hail Mary is an effective method of calling on Mary for several reasons. For one, it is a prayer that honors her. More importantly, it focuses on the Incarnation of God in the human person of Jesus. Mary is *full of grace* and *blessed among women* because of her relation to Jesus. We go to Mary ultimately to use her as a pathway to Christ. She always leads us to her son.

The Hail Mary begins with two events in Mary's life that are found in Scripture. *Hail Mary full of grace, the Lord is with you,* is the greeting from Angel Gabriel to Mary at the Annunciation. Gabriel told Mary that she would conceive Jesus, the Messiah. This event is found in the Gospel of Luke, Chapter One.

Blessed art you among women, and blessed is the fruit of your womb, Jesus, is the greeting from Mary's cousin Elizabeth at the Visitation. Also in the Gospel of Luke, we learn that Elizabeth conceived far beyond the age anyone was thought to be capable of bearing a child. Both Mary's and Elizabeth's pregnancies illustrate that nothing is impossible with God.

The second half of the Hail Mary, *Holy Mary, Mother of God, pray for us sinners now and at the hour of our death, Amen,* is a petition. It is a request for Mary to help us at this very moment and in anticipation of our eternity with Christ. We ask for her assistance and guidance in this life and into the next.

🙞 🙜

Why Pray to Mary?

Mary has maintained a significant level of popularity since her earthly life. More art, literature and music are dedicated to her than any other woman in history. Her name is affectionately called on every continent of the planet. Her image is displayed on everything from lighters and bumper stickers to rosaries and priceless works of art.

She is honored on her feast days and remembered in the liturgy. Public and private shrines are erected in her honor worldwide. And pilgrims travel hundreds, sometimes thousands, of miles to places where she appeared so they may feel closer to her.

If you are not yet a devotee of Mary you may wonder why so many people go to such an extent for her. What is it about her that prompts followers to be so very fond of her ever since she first walked this earth? You also may ask why we go to her rather than directly to God the Father, her son Jesus, or the Holy Spirit.

Once you are aware of Mary's presence in your life and feel the warmth of her love, you will understand. No doubt you too will fall in love with this incredible saint and discover for yourself why for nearly two thousand years people have known that not only does God care for us, our heavenly mother cares deeply for us as well. When we are hurting, we can go to her for love and support as well as answers. Mary will assist us in our time of need. All it takes is a simple request.

✂ ✄

Grieving with Mary

While we are often blessed with joy, the human condition is sometimes one of conflict and tribulation. Grief is unavoidable. Everyone encounters heartache at one point or another. We battle our addictions and abuses. We disagree and argue with family, friends and coworkers. We suffer from illness and the loss of loved ones. We stress over finances and employment issues.

During such times, much comfort is found from our faith. We gain hope that our prayers are answered in the goodness and mercy of the Lord. We also attain peace in the support of saints and angels with whom God surrounds us. For many of us, Mary, who is the greatest of all the saints, is particularly comforting.

This form of relief is more likely found if we have a pre-existing belief system prior to a crisis. Once we're in the heat of things, our heads buzz with a mixture of thoughts, making prayer more difficult for even the strongest believers. It then is more challenging to realize God's loving hand in all aspects of our life—even those that are troubling.

Grieving triggers a range of spiritual questions. We

ask why "this" happened to us. Why did it happen now? We want to know why we must endure such anguish and how long must we suffer.

When our security is threatened, it's not unusual to begin a dance with God. We bargain that we will do something if God does something for us. If we don't get what we want, emotions may turn to anger. We blame God for the evil done by human beings or for not preventing bad things from touching us. We think God did not answer our prayer, when in reality our answer came but differed from our expectations.

Leaning on Mary shouldn't result in such feelings. Mary doesn't possess the authority to grant miracles, so we really can't hold her responsible. God is the only one who answers prayers. When we pray to Mary, or any other saints, we simply are asking for their intercession. Prayer is a plea for help. It is a request for the one to whom we pray to take our prayers to God, to support us in our quest for answers.

Scripture instructs us to petition prayers from, and pray for, one another (see Thessalonians 2, 3:1-2). We solicit prayers from Mary the same way we ask for prayers from our friends and family. Everyone belongs to God's family of humans. We all are united in Christ, "so we, who are many, are one body in Christ, and individually we are members one of another" (Romans 12:5).

God is the ultimate healer and the only one we worship. Praying to Mary does not replace our adoration of

God but rather promotes a greater devotion to God. The Second Vatican Council's Constitution on the Church affirms this by stating that the maternal role of Mary in no way obscures or diminishes the unique mediation of Christ, but rather shows its power (#60).

However, Mary does reign in an influential position. As Jesus is King, and Mary is his mother, she is queen of heaven and earth and the one person by whom he most likely is influenced. When we bring our troubles to Mary, we ask that she then ask the Lord, along with us, to solve our problems as we hope. And we can confidently trust that is exactly what she will do because of her great unconditional mother's love for all of us.

A journey to Mary is a circle of joy and love that flows to her and from her. She is a fine example of humility, hope and faith. Mary was "highly favored" by God and recognized for her goodness (see Luke 1:28, 1:42, 1:48). She is our role model, teacher, protector and advocate. We strive to serve, trust and respond to God as she did. Therefore, praying to her leads us closer to God.

We love Mary in the way that Jesus does. We may assume that, while on earth as a devout Jew, Jesus followed the commandments and honored Mary because she was his mother. We are to do the same, given that she is our mother as well. Recognizing Mary as the mother of the world is an ancient tradition dating back to the first centuries. This stems from the knowledge that Jesus shared her with us from the cross when he instructed Mary and his disciple, John: "Woman, here is your Son," and told John, "Here is your Mother" (John 19:27).

We can depend on Mary to help us in our need. She stays closest to us, her children, when we are in crisis, as all good mothers do. She knows our pain, because she, like us, lived a human life and experienced struggles as great as any of us. She patiently listens to all of our deepest desires and concerns. We may rest assured that if we place our troubles in her hands, she will take them to her son.

Mary's concern is for our health, well-being, and most of all, our relationship with her son. She prays for our continuous conversion, always taking us to Jesus, who takes us to the Father. Mary said, "My soul magnifies the Lord and my Spirit has rejoiced in God my Savior" (Luke 1:46-55). Mary encourages us to give glory to the Father, follow her son, and let the Spirit transform us.

☘ ☘

Our Prayer Intentions
Prayer is an opportunity for communication with the divine and the holy. When we pray to Mary, we are talking with her. We may pray to ask something of her, honor her, or simply be close to our friend and mother. She listens to us, and hopefully, we listen to her. We trust that, after praying, we will be guided and inspired by her. Our choices and any action we take should be influenced by her.

There are many reasons for us to pray. Most often, we do so because we are in need. We go running to God or to Mary when we are frightened, sick, worried or tired. We seek peace while journeying through the turbulent waters of our lives. We also give thanks to God and Mary for their assistance.

By the example of how she lived her life, and when appearing to people through the centuries, Mary taught us how to pray and gave us suggestions for what to pray for. When Our Lady appeared to the children of Fatima, Portugal, she asked us to pray for the conversion of sinners. Few of us consider praying for conversion, but if we all work to move closer to God, we will progress to a more peaceful world. We won't hurt ourselves or others if God is first in our lives and we see God's reflection in every human being.

We also can pray for an increase in faith. That trust and assurance in God's mercy and generosity is tested when we suffer. Those strong in their faith may encounter doubts from time to time but do find peace in their belief that God remains with them always. On the other hand, those who have no faith struggle to find it when they need it most. They may feel guilty or incompetent in their ability to connect with God when they hadn't previously done so on happier occasions.

Probably the most common reason we run to our heavenly mother is for physical healing. When we, or someone we love, are sick, we turn to Mary in prayer.

We ask her to pray for us, to pray our prayer. This is exactly what Scripture tells us to do. We are instructed to ask people to pray in this way: "Are any among you sick? They should call for the elders of the church and have them pray over them" (James 5:14). And when we are hurting from the loss of someone or something, Mary fills the empty spaces in our hearts with her love. Our prayers are answered with her tenderness.

We know from Scripture that nothing is impossible with God. There is no limit to the miraculous gifts God bestows on us. Miracles happen every day in every way, and Mary's intercession is extremely powerful. People who pray to her emphatically declare that she assists with their prayers being answered.

However, it is important to remember that, although countless physical healings and other answered prayers are attributed to Mary's intercession, not all prayers are answered in the way we anticipate. The healings resulting from faith and prayer to her are most often of a spiritual nature. Prayer typically is an additional remedy in the healing process. Modern physical and psychological medicine should still be sought along with the presence, touch, and supportive words of a live human being. In fact, these elements of healing may well be part of the answer to our prayers.

✄ ✄

Your Devotion to Mary

There are many ways to show devotion, many ways to pray. Your journey to Mary is as individual as you are. There are no rules when praying to her. No one way is better than another. Mary listens to all prayers, whether they are crude or refined, simple or elaborate, silent or aloud.

You can pray alone or with friends. Some gather strength by praying traditional prayers the way they have been said for centuries. Others speak to her in their own words. There are admirers of Mary who dedicate their entire lives to caring for the hungry and needy in her name or promise to pray her intentions daily. Other followers show their devotion musically or by sculpturing and painting. And pilgrims trek thousands of miles at great financial expense to honor her at shrines around the world.

Whichever way you choose to honor Mary, one thing is very likely: You will become more aware of her presence. Whether you feel it or not, you will know that she is with you, watching over you, protecting you, and ready to help. When sad or hurt, her tenderness will warm your heart. You will feel God's gift of Mary's sweet love. More significantly, your love for Jesus also will grow in ways you could not have imagined.

Chapter One

Santo Domingo Rosary Chapel.
Puebla, Mexico.

Devotion with Words

"Remember O most gracious Virgin Mary, that never was it known that anyone who fled to your protection, implored your help, or sought your intercession was left unaided." These are the first words of the prayer known as the *Memorare*. Written in medieval times by St. Bernard of Clairvaux, the prayer declares confidence in the powerful intercession of Mary.

Prayer simply is a conversation with a heavenly friend, whether it is God, a saint, or an angel. Mary has topped the list as a favorite prayer target for nearly two thousand years. Some prayers are intended to honor her, but most ask her to pray for us. It is our way of pleading for her assistance in our time of need. When we are in pain, or when we feel sorrowful, anxious or lonely, we can rest assured that Jesus' mother, who is our heavenly mother, is eager to listen and help us.

In addition to talking with family, friends, and professional counselors, verbal prayer helps us put our pain into words. This is an important element in grief recovery. Even when no one seems to listen or care, we can go to God—and Mary and the saints who then go to

God on our behalf—and trust that we are heard. We can voice our pain to them with spontaneous or traditional prayers written, spoken or sung.

When grieving, some people prefer to utilize what already is familiar to them. There is security in going to places we know, being with close friends, and engaging in routine activities. We also gain comfort from saying a prayer we remember from happier days. But there are so many prayers from which to choose that, if we look, we may come across a different one that expresses our feelings more clearly.

These prayers are available in hundreds of books, on holy cards, and on countless websites. *Little Office of the Blessed Virgin Mary* is a very useful book for those who are devoted to Mary. In this book you will find readings, hymns, psalms and prayers to Mary for morning and evening of each day of the week. This extensive collection began as a part of the Roman Breviary and is modeled after the Divine Office, which is a collection of prayers prayed daily by priests and others.

❧ ❧

Prayers to Mary
The *Sub tuum praesidium* is the oldest known Marian prayer. Written in Greek on Egyptian papyrus, the ancient prayer is estimated to date to the third century. *Sub tuum* is indicative of the early Christian's level of confidence in Mary's intercession. This confidence continues

today. In addition to being prayed by the general laity, it
is recited at the end of the Divine Office and in Ambro-
sian, Roman, Byzantine and Coptic liturgies.

The little prayer is quite perfect in expressing our basic
human desires. You may wish to memorize and repeat it
daily or write it down and keep it on hand, perhaps in a
wallet, purse, or on your desk. When you are anxious or
troubled, you may pray:

We turn to you for protection,
Holy Mother of God.
Listen to our prayers,
And help us in our needs.
Save us from every danger,
Glorious and blessed Virgin.

Other popular prayers to Mary include the *Magnifi-*
cat, which comes from Mary's Song of Praise (see Luke
1:46-55); the *Hail Holy Queen*, which is a Marian hymn
from the eleventh or twelfth century and is prayed at
the end of the rosary and in the Liturgy of the Hours;
the *Angelus*, which is prayed morning, noon and evening; and the *Litany of the Blessed Virgin Mary*, a prayer
that names Our Lady in countless ways.

A special prayer form that is recited for nine consecu-
tive days is known as a novena. Novenas may consist of
one prayer or a group of prayers. They often are prayed
during times of grief because novenas are believed to

be so effective. As early as the first millennium, people prayed novenas in remembrance of the nine days between the Ascension of Our Lord and the descent of the Holy Spirit on Pentecost. Some people publicly acknowledge their appreciation for an answer to their novena by publishing their thanksgiving in magazines and newspapers.

Another special prayer is *The Seven Sorrows of Mary*, which focuses on the saddest events of Mary's life. We pray to Mary in our times of need because we know she understands our deepest concerns. She was a wife, mother and widow and experienced loss and heartache in those roles. The events in Mary's life on which we meditate with *The Seven Sorrows of Mary* include:

1) *The Prophecy of Simeon* (see Luke 2:1-35). When Mary and Joseph first took the infant Jesus to the temple to present him to the Lord, the righteous man named Simeon forewarned Mary of events to come. He told Mary that her child was destined for the falling and rising of many and that a sword would (symbolically) pierce her soul as well.

2) *The Flight into Egypt* (see Matthew 2:13-18). An angel appeared to Joseph in a dream and told him that King Herod was searching for Jesus with the intention of destroying him. The angel instructed Joseph to take his family to Egypt immediately, and so the Holy Family quickly fled from the comforts of their home to protect their son.

3) *The Three Days Young Jesus was Lost* (see Luke 2:41-51). When Jesus was twelve years old, Mary, Joseph, Jesus, and their extended family celebrated the festival of Passover in Jerusalem. On their way home Mary and Joseph realized that Jesus was not with other relatives as they thought. The alarmed parents hurried back to Jerusalem. After three days of traveling and searching, they found their son in the temple with the teachers.

4) *Watching Jesus Carry the Cross* (see Luke 23:26-31). Many people witnessed the badly-beaten Jesus struggling to carry the cross on which he was to hang. Undoubtedly, Mary was there also to be near her beloved son in his last hours. She then, in great anguish, watched her son's degradation, torture and pain.

5) *The Crucifixion* (see John 19:25-27). Crucifixion was a deliberately humiliating and excruciatingly painful sentence for anyone. No doubt, Mary suffered greatly witnessing the death of her dear son in such a manner.

6) *Removal of Jesus' Body from the Cross* (see Luke 23:50-53). After Jesus died, they removed his limp body from the cross and returned him to Mary. We can only imagine the anger and helplessness Mary felt seeing her child die as Jesus did. Her grief was overwhelming.

7) *Jesus Being Laid in the Tomb* (see Luke 23:50-56). After great suffering, we feel both relief and sadness when death takes our loved ones. We are relieved that the pain is over for them but saddened by the finality of their death. Mary most likely experienced a similar

dichotomy of emotions when she laid Jesus' body in the tomb and watched the heavy stone roll in place to seal its entrance.

⚜ ⚜

Devotional Reading on Mary

Reading about the gentle, yet strong, Mary is inspiring and very helpful in working through our struggles. From devotional writings on Mary, not only do we come to know her better, we also discover how we too may answer God's call while moving through our own troubles. We learn, ponder and develop new and clearer thoughts by reading about the woman who carried and raised the savior of the world.

When we are faced with uncertainty, we have Mary's example to follow. She handled her life challenges as a perfect model of faith. Mary did not lead a privileged life. She experienced many trying and even dangerous situations. However, she put her trust in God and submitted to God's will.

Following Mary's model can be challenging. It is effortless to love and honor God in happy times; stressful and sorrowful times are quite another matter. Relinquishing control to God, or at the very least our illusion of ever having control, when our world seems so unsettled is definitely not easy to do. But that is what faith is all about.

What we know of Mary's human life on earth comes

from a variety of sources including the Bible, writings by the Fathers of the Church and other faith-filled authors, legends, and stories of personal encounters with her spirit. Some are trusted works. Others we must read carefully and with the understanding that, although thought-provoking, little factual content exists for them.

From this array of writings it is believed that Mary lived much like other devout Jewish women of her time. She abided by the Hebrew teachings and traditions handed down to her through generations. In addition, bearing in mind that God entrusted her with the responsibility of carrying and raising his beloved son, we know Mary was good, loving, and incredibly special in the Lord's eyes. She had to be the perfect model of faith to be chosen as the mother of Jesus.

Many of the early writings on Mary are considered apocrypha, which comes from the Greek word meaning "hidden." Although a respected prophet or apostle wrote this literature, it is not necessarily considered divinely inspired. One apocryphal book called the "Protoevangelium"—or Gospel of James—is fascinating to read. This book features stories of Mary's childhood, her marriage to Joseph, the birth of Jesus, and Mary's adult life. However, written around 150 A.D., the "Protoevangelium" is deemed more legendary than factual, because it is uncertain which elements of the book were common knowledge at the time and which the writer fabricated.

The "Protoevangelium" tells of the elderly couple, Joachim and Anne, who are traditionally recognized as Mary's parents. From this source and others, it is thought that Mary was born about 20 B.C. in the village of Nazareth in Galilee or near the Sheep's Gate in Jerusalem. Her parents gave her the Hebrew name of Miriam, which is translated as "Hope" or "Star of the Sea." The name was popular at the time of Mary's birth because Moses' sister, who was a prophet, was also named Miriam.

The Bible is the most reliable source on Mary. But even here, details are limited. The Gospels of Matthew and especially Luke tell of events that involve Mary and address her by name, which was unusual for the time in which they were written. Women were not commonly named specifically in any writing, so it is no surprise that Mary's name is used infrequently. Most often she is referred to as the mother of Jesus, or "woman," a term of respect used at that time. Besides, the public knew very well who Mary was. They didn't need her name spelled out for them.

The most specific stories in the scriptures involving Mary are found in the Gospel of Luke. These chapters include the Annunciation (see 1:26-38), her visit with Elizabeth (see 1:39-45), Mary's Song of Praise (see 1:46-55), the nativity (see 2:6-7), the presentation (see 2:22-38), and the finding of Jesus in the temple (see 2:41-51). Also of significance is the wedding in Cana described in the Gospel of John (see 2:1-12). In addition, much is learned about Mary from some of the stories of Christ which refer to her indirectly, such as when authors addressed Mary as Jesus' mother.

⚜ ⚜

Mary's Life Challenges

Reading these stories we realize that, although our situations are not identical, we can relate to Mary's trials and she can understand ours. She is the greatest of all saints, but she knows exactly how we feel. She identifies with our pain because her heartaches were at least as great as ours.

We can only imagine how Mary, as a young teenager, accepted the honors and challenges of being chosen by God to be the mother of Jesus, the savior of the world. We know that when told, she proclaimed the glory of God. She probably did not fully understand how she was to conceive the Messiah or how that role might impact her life, but she trusted God. She placed her worries into the hands of the Lord.

Mary's pregnancy put her in a very complicated situation. If a woman became pregnant before marriage, as she did, the custom was to condemn her to death by stoning. When Joseph discovered Mary's pregnancy, he decided to discretely call off the engagement to avoid such a sentence. An angel intervened by appearing to Joseph in a dream and telling him not to be afraid to take

Mary as his wife. We know Joseph did indeed follow the angel's guidance.

When Mary was in her late pregnancy, she and Joseph journeyed to Bethlehem, in accordance with the decree by the Emperor Augustus, to participate in a census. In the city of David, far from her own home, Mary gave birth to Jesus in a crude stable. Scripture also tells us of the visit from the wise men, Jesus' circumcision, the prediction made by Simeon, and the family's terrifying flight into Egypt after a warning from an angel that Jesus' safety was in danger. Throughout it all, as a good Hebrew mother, Mary raised her son in the Jewish faith, fully knowing God and God's relationship with the chosen people. The holy family also participated in Jewish traditions and practices including the observance of the Passover Feast.

From then on, we know little of Mary's life until Jesus' ministry days and crucifixion and her participation in the closed room where the Holy Spirit descended upon her and the disciples. After Jesus' resurrection and ascension, it is believed that Mary continued to pray, preach the teachings of her son, and reside with the disciple John in Jerusalem or Ephesus until the end of her life on earth.

What does Mary's life, her example of faith, mean to us as Christians? By reading about the events she experienced, we realize the struggle and tragedy she faced. Imagine her concerns over the unusual conception, giv-

ing birth in a strange city in unsanitary conditions and
without basic comforts, and fleeing with her family to
Egypt to protect her child. More troubling, Mary probably prayed incessantly when she realized the tension
growing over her son's ministry and during his trial,
persecution and crucifixion.

Mary certainly didn't receive the answer to her des-
perate prayer—that Jesus' life be spared. We only may
guess by her character that she continued to trust God's
reasoning for it all. In her grief and sorrow there is no
doubt that she put her faith in God.

※ ※

Other Sources

Other works of interest about Mary include those written
by early theologians and the Fathers of our Church, which
are the early defenders and writers of our faith. These men
contemplated Mary's role as mother of Jesus and her participation in the process of salvation. For example, Ori-
gen (d. 254) is thought to be the first to use the term
Theotokos, which means "God-bearer." Others referred to
Mary as the Ark of the Covenant. The correlation is drawn
from the comparison of the ark, which is the container
that Moses built to hold the tablets of the Ten Commandments and therefore believed to be the dwelling-place of
God, and Mary's body, which was the dwelling place of
the fetus of God in the human person of Jesus.

Hundreds of books written by clergy, religious men

and women, and laity are available on Mary as well. Many are excellent. Others, although written with devotion, are more affectionate than substantive or theologically grounded. As stated previously, for this reason, readers should take some caution when selecting books to read. It's important to consider the credibility of the author and publisher. (For a good overall handbook on Mary, pick up *The Catholic Companion to Mary* by Sister Mary Kathleen Glavich.)

In addition, from Church documents we learn solid information on proper devotion to Mary and her position in our faith. A good place to begin reading is the chapter titled "Constitution on the Church" of the Vatican Council II documents and references to Mary in the *Catechism of the Catholic Church*, a handbook recommended for all Catholic households. Also of interest are documents written by several popes including:

- "*Marialis Cultus*: For the Right Ordering and Development of Devotion to the Blessed Virgin Mary" dated February 2, 1974 by Pope Paul VI
- "*Redemptoris Mater* (The Mother of the Redeemer): On the Blessed Virgin Mary in the Life of the Pilgrim Church," which is the encyclical letter dated March 25, 1987 by Pope John Paul II
- "*Rosarium Virginis Mariae*: On the Most Holy Rosary," the apostolic letter dated October 16, 2002 by Pope John Paul II

Although lengthy, these documents are quite readable, interesting and informative. You can find copies of them in some books, such as *Mary in the Church* by the United States Conference of Catholic Bishops, and on the Holy See (Vatican) website at www.vatican.va.

᙮ ᙭

Holy Mary

Mary offers a perfect example of how we may trust in the Lord during life's struggles and live in such a way that leads us to an eternity with Christ. Her purity was present upon her conception. She is the only human conceived without the stain of Original Sin—a mark passed on to us as a result of the actions of Adam and Eve. Her Immaculate Conception was told in early Christian hymns and writings by many saints including Saint Ambrose and Saint Augustine. Pope Pius X officially proclaimed this truth in the dogma of the Immaculate Conception in a bull titled, *Ineffabilis Deus*, on December 8, 1854.

It is believed that Mary's purity continued throughout her life. The angel Gabriel said that the Lord was with her and that she found favor with God. For this reason the Eastern Orthodox Churches honor Mary with the title *Panagia*, which means the "All-Holy." This level of holiness ties in with the belief in her life-long virginity, which is a topic of considerable debate between different Christian faiths. Little doubt exists that Mary was a virgin when she gave birth to Jesus. In addition, the Catholic and Orthodox churches teach that Mary remained celibate after Jesus' birth.

As a result of her purity and role as mother of Jesus, it also is believed that at the end of Mary's earthly life her body and soul were simultaneously assumed—taken up—into heaven by God. The belief is rooted in tradition and depicted in early Christian writings, hymns and icons based on several factors. For one, Mary is not the only one who was assumed. God took the prophets Enoch (Hebrews 11:5) and Elijah (2 Kings 2:11) into heaven this way. In addition, no tomb or remains of Mary's body were ever found. Had remains been found, every church in Europe and the Middle East would boast of owning a fragment of her bones.(Displaying bone fragments of saints, known as relics, in a decorative holder—reliquary—is a common method of honoring canonized saints in the Catholic Church.)

The celebration of the feast of Mary's assumption extends back to the sixth century. In 1950 Pope Pius XII filed the bull *Munificentissimus Deus*. The document officially mandates belief in her assumption as an element of the Catholic faith. We celebrate the feast of Mary's Assumption in the liturgy each year on August 15.

Mary's assumption is of great importance to us because it is indicative of what we, and all those we know and love, will experience when Jesus comes again at the end of times. We will not be assumed with our body into heaven as Mary was assumed. However, if we do our best to avoid sin—which is the deliberate turning away from God—when we die our soul will separate from our body and go to heaven. Then, on the last day—which is the end of the world as we know it—Christ will raise our bodies and reunite them with our souls.

The belief in the resurrection of the body is one of our basic Christian truths. We declare it to be so at the end of the prayers *The Apostles' Creed* and *The Nicene Creed*, which we pray during Mass. More importantly, there also is reference to this truth in Scripture, "If the Spirit of him who raised Jesus from the dead dwells in you, he who raised Christ from the dead will give life to your mortal bodies also through his Spirit that dwells in you" (Romans 8:11).

The death of a loved one raises questions of their whereabouts and our own mortality. Death is inevitable. At some point we, and every other human being, will leave this world for what Christians believe is a better life—an eternity in heaven with Christ. We take comfort in knowing that if we, and our loved ones, live a life that is pleasing to God, we not only will see God upon our death, we will unite with our friends and relatives again as well, in body and soul, at the end of times.

※ ※

Muslim Devotion to Mary

Christians and Muslims have experienced numerous conflicts between them through the centuries but share belief in one true God and an important devotion to

Mary. Many Christians may find it surprising that the Koran, which is the holy book for Islam, gives a detailed account of Mary's life from the viewpoint of the Islamic faith. Although the Koran is not recommended reading for Christians, it is interesting to know that in it Mary is the only woman mentioned indirectly or by name, and she is named more than forty times. The Koran tells the story of Mary's Immaculate Conception, dedication to the Lord, and her life and role as the mother of Jesus in detail. Called Sitna Miriam, she is recognized as a saintly woman and honored for her purity, virginity and obedience to God.

Muslims believe several Marian apparitions—appearances of Mary's spirit—relate to them as well as Christians. They feel a strong connection to her for this reason. For example, when Mary appeared to Juan Diego in Mexico in 1531, Mary stood upon a crescent moon, which is a symbol of Islam. Therefore, Muslims believed Mary gave the Islamic community an important and personal sign.

More significant is the story of the apparitions that took place in Fatima, Portugal. The Moors originally named the city of Fatima after Mohammed's favorite daughter. The princess of the nearby Castle of Ourem, who converted to Catholicism before her death, also was named Fatima. When Mary appeared to the children of Fatima in 1917, Muslims felt she connected with them too. After all, their Sitna Miriam blessed the city of their honored Fatima. For these reasons, many Muslims make pilgrimages to Fatima in honor of Mary and in memory of Mohammed's daughter.

From these apparitions we see that Mary desperately attempts to reach all people. Her messages are not intended for an isolated, privileged group. She loves all of us equally and desires every one of her children to love one another and continue to move closer to her son. In our greatest need and sorrow we stand together as a world community, wrapped in our heavenly mother's arms, under one God.

⚜ ⚜

Words of Prayer Put to Music

There is a saying that on Sunday mornings people may not remember the homily but will leave the church humming the hymns. Music is a passionate method of prayer because it is a sensual means of expression, utilizing at least three of the five senses—sight, sound and touch. (We use our sight by reading the music and *seeing* it being played or sung; we *hear* the music; we *feel* its vibration and *hold* the songbook in our hands.)

Medical teams across the country are discovering the therapeutic effect of music on patients with physical and psychological needs. Music therapy is found to comfort seriously distressed, ill and dying patients of all ages, from the very young to the very old. During therapeutic sessions, an individualized musical formula is administered by degreed practitioners. The impressive results show that the therapy promotes wellness, manages stress and pain, and enhances memory.

For many of those who are fond of Mary, Marian music is the prescription of choice. Music therapists armed with guitars and harps sing Marian hymns to patients in hospitals and medical centers across the country. Most of the songs are light and sweet as our heavenly mother. Like lullabies, singing or listening to them not only can soothe the soul on a sad day but also lift us higher on a good one.

If you do not have the advantage of listening to a singer in person, pick up a CD of Marian music. The hymns offer a gentle alternative to television and radio. Hundreds of hymns are available in a wide range of languages. Some are the familiar songs we sing in church. Others are favorites of generations past.

The history and evolution of many of these songs is interesting to note. Several Marian hymns began as a prayer. Others are more often read today than sung as originally intended. During the nineteenth and twentieth centuries, Marian hymns reigned as an integral part of Catholic celebration. Today, we rarely sing them at Mass unless it is a Marian feast day.

As a result, these songs are not very familiar to the younger generations. Although still popular, but in a more limited way, songs such as *Lovely Lady Dressed in Blue, On This Day O Beautiful Mother*, and *O Queen of the Rosary* are reminiscent of May crownings and weddings decades ago.

Stabat Mater, which means "the Mother was Standing" in Latin, is a thirteenth century Marian hymn that expresses Mary's anguish watching her son at the cross. The lyrics also ask that we are filled with Christ's love and unite Mary's suffering with ours. More than sixty English translations are known for this hymn.

A few other hymns plead for Mary's assistance. Seldom sung today, *Mother Dear, O Pray for Me* asks Mary for protection during difficult times. This centuries-old musical prayer is indicative of the devotion to Mary that the faithful maintained in times of need.

Mary Did You Know; Immaculate Mary; Hail, Holy Queen Enthroned Above; and *Gentle Woman* are more popular, contemporary Marian hymns. However, many of the classical ones, such as Schubert's and Giuseppe Verdi's versions of *Ave Maria*, continue to be important elements of celebration during the Christmas season.

Pope John Paul II listed three characteristics of sacred music: its sanctity, true art, and universality—meaning that the music is holy, creative, and for everyone. Sacred music presents a belief in a way that touches people of differing languages and customs at our very core, regardless of our ethnicity, gender or age.

❧ ☙

Putting Your Prayers into Words

We can confidently go to Mary with our problems knowing she understands and cares about us. Without a doubt, she brings our prayers to her son. You may pray traditional prayers; sing, play or listen to songs and hymns; and read or write articles and books on Mary. You also may talk to Mary in your own words, speaking from your heart.

If writing your thoughts is easier for you than verbalizing them, a prayer journal may be a good option. Pick up a notebook and write a letter to Mary after a special occasion. You also may wish simply to jot down your daily thoughts. Your notes need not be well-written. Merely make a list or write a letter as if you were writing to a loved one. You may wish to do this first thing in the morning or just before bedtime each evening. Or if you want to say something specific to Mary at the start or end of each day, write this message on an index card or slip of paper and keep it handy in your wallet, on your desk, or on the refrigerator.

When you are lonely, tired or troubled, ask our heavenly mother to come closer to you. Call on her with words you feel most comfortable using. Whatever way you choose, Mary will pray your prayers with you.

Chapter Two

National Museum of Art.
Washington, D.C.

Devotion through Art

Sandro Botticelli, Raphael, Michelangelo, Francesco Botticini, Caravaggio, Rembrandt, Mary Cassatt and Salvador Dali. The world's greatest fine artists, along with thousands who are lesser known, felt the need to reveal their vision of the Virgin Mary through art. Whether painted with oil on canvas or carved in marble, more artwork has been created of Mary than any other woman in history.

From the first century, patrons displayed paintings and statues of Our Lady in courtyards, churches and homes and carried them into battle. These representations honor her and plea for assistance. Devotees feel her image promotes a sense of protection. It is a sign that our loving mother is watching over us. Look to the streets of Rome for such an example and you will see a portrait of Mary displayed in most city squares. Romans believe that, when under her watchful eye, it is safe to walk the streets and sleep peacefully at night.

Marian art also offers solace in times of loss. For those who are suddenly alone, a figurine or portrait of Mary serves as a reminder that she is with us. In the midst of our sorrow, our holy mother holds us close.

You even may wish to create your own Marian work of art. The prayerful process of creation incorporates the therapeutic benefits of recognizing and illustrating our emotional concerns with the spiritual benefits of placing them in Mary's—and ultimately God's—hands. If you find it difficult to do this, call on Mary. She will help you draw through and out of the pain. You may or may not feel her physical presence, but you can trust that she is with you.

For some time, the practice of creating art was known to promote healing, but it did not emerge as a distinct therapy until the 1940s. Traditional medical professionals now know that a special type of therapeutic art, directed under the eye of a degreed and accredited therapist, facilitates mental and physical healing. Hospitals, clinics, and treatment centers use art therapy to enable patients to articulate their thoughts and feelings in a way they could not otherwise, which is an important step in moving through the grieving process. Sometimes we do not recognize our own emotions until we see them revealed in colors and shapes on paper. And when this therapy is combined with prayer, the possibility of healing spiritually is likely.

❧ ❧

Devotional Art
Fine art and sculpture relay entire stories without using words. When we first glance at a painting or carving

we see an object, person or landscape. Once we look deeper into the artwork we find a story waiting to be told. Through the perception of the artist we experience an event, personality or emotion.

Although artists express their impressions and perceptions on a wide range of levels, devotional art in its true form tells stories based on sound theological beliefs. The artwork shows the teachings of Scripture and the Church as clearly as spoken or written words tell them. Sometimes the work is considered sacred by believers.

Viewing artwork often raises us to a new level of awareness. It is a source of inspiration and consolation that may touch us by bringing us to tears, laughter, confusion, awe or reverence. Like a healing tonic, its beauty and meaning soothe an aching heart.

Periodically throughout history, debates surrounded the reverence awarded divine art. Some of these deliberations resulted in drastic measures against it. Scripture verses from both Exodus (20:4) and Deuteronomy (5:8-9) forbid the creation of idols. During the sixteenth century, because of Martin Luther's interpretations of the biblical passages and resulting reforms, not only was religious visual art production minimal, but fanatics destroyed much of the centuries-old, priceless and irreplaceable pieces.

However, it is important to note that the devotional art from Orthodox and Catholic traditions is not viewed as idols by the faithful. Homage is not paid to the statues or paintings. The objects are tools to facilitate meditating on the event or person portrayed. It is much like displaying photos of family members in a home or carrying them in a wallet. No one believes the photograph is actually the person; no one has feelings for the paper photograph. The picture merely promotes warm and loving thoughts of the person photographed and assists with prayerful communication.

The second Council of Nicaea in the year 787 A.D. made this essential distinction. The Council determined that veneration in the presence of statues is acceptable. Devotional art serves as a powerful reminder of holy people and the sacrifices they made out of love for God. They are an inspiration for us to serve the Lord following the saints' examples.

Modern churches are careful with placement of representations of Mary and the saints. Devotional art is never to detract attention from divine adoration. The focus, especially on the altar, is on the Trinity. In keeping with this understanding, Pope John Paul II mandated in the Code of Canon Law, 1983: "Images should be displayed in moderate numbers and in suitable fashion."

※ ※

Marian Art through the Ages
Legend says that Mary posed with the infant Jesus in her arms for a portrait by St. Luke. The oldest known image of Mary is on a wall in the catacomb of St. Priscilla in

Rome. The drawing is thought to date to the late second century. Others in the catacombs of Petrus and Marcellianus, also in Rome, are believed to date to the third century.

Throughout history, Marian art reflected the times as well as society's current relationship with the Mother of God. Artistic representations of Mary vary with the ethnicity of the artist, the current perception of Mary, fashion trends, and the Church's latest decree. Mary's portrayals include an innocent young woman, mother of the infant or child Jesus, and royal queen. She's appeared common and regal. Her skin tones and features reflect people of various cultures including Caucasian, Asian, Native American, East Indian and African.

Fine art may take six months to a year or more to complete. Although only a fraction of the time one takes to grieve, this is a tremendous investment on the part of the artist. Yet foremost in the hearts of so many artists is the need to be close to Mary that century after century they have used their time and talent to honor her through their art. Through their chosen medium they speak to and pray with Mary, and by doing so they offer opportunities for admirers of their work to connect with her as well.

An evolution of thought is seen by the type of art produced through the ages. When the Council of Ephesus in the year 431 declared Mary the *Theotokos*—the Mother of God—representations of mother and child increased in popularity. Around the year 600, the Eastern Church designated August 15 as the Feast of the Dormition, now known as the Feast of the Assumption. Artists then portrayed Mary falling asleep, often in the presence of saints with Jesus ready to take her to heaven.

In the ancient city of Byzantium, which was later known as Constantinople and then Istanbul, Mary was regally depicted. This portrayal signified her power as greater than the rulers. European royalty followed by ordering artists to portray them in the popular Marian images to divert reverence from her to them.

During the late 1300s and early 1400s, Mary's regal image shifted to the loving and sorrowful mother due to the number of children who died in the plague. The greatest cause of heartache for any parents, or expectant parents, is their children's suffering, illness, dangerous behavior, or death. Parents expect to see their children live healthy and happy lives long beyond them.

When a child dies in birth or during childhood, not only does the family lose a cherished family member, it also loses part of its innocence and purity. Future joys parents may have hoped to experience with the child are no longer possible. In addition, the parents experience a type of death themselves as part of their legacy dies with the child. Their roles and definitions of themselves as parents are forever changed.

This pain was expressed in medieval Marian art. Mothers sympathized with Mary's love for her child and her mourning over Jesus' pain and death. They knew that Mary understood their own suffering. She could identify with their intense grief, and they identified with hers. For this reason, pietas—representations of the sorrowful mother with Jesus after the crucifixion—which were popular from at least the eleventh century, became even more so.

Michelangelo's sculpture is the most famous pieta. It also is the most frequently viewed work of devotional art in the world. Showcased behind bulletproof glass in St. Peter's Basilica in the Vatican, the magnificent sculpture draws countless admirers each year. Completed in 1498 when Michelangelo was only twenty-four years old, the pieta masterfully reveals the full humanity of the divine Jesus as well as the magnitude of Mary's love for her son and her great sorrow over his death.

In the mid-1500s the Council of Trent forbade images representing false doctrines. Paintings that depicted Mary in ways that were not specifically known to be biblically founded were removed from the churches. Because Mary is only directly referred to in a handful of Scriptural passages, devotional art could only depict particular events. Accepted topics included the Annunciation (see Luke 1:26-38), Visitation (see Luke 1:39-56), Nativity (see Luke 2:1-7) the Flight into Egypt (see Matthew 2:13-15), standing at the foot of the cross (see Luke 19:25-27), and her presence in the upper room for the Pentecost (see Acts 1:12-2:4).

The most popular of these events was the Annunciation—when the Angel Gabriel appeared to Mary and told her she would bear a son named Jesus. In many of these portraits, Mary is shown with Gabriel kneeling before her or looming over her. Sometimes she holds a lily with three blossoms to symbolize her virginity before, during and after Jesus' birth. The Holy Spirit looms over her as a ray of light or a dove.

To some degree, the use of symbolism in art parallels grief and loss. When grieving, we look for symbols to remind us that our loved one is still with us. We gain comfort in the symbols of the love and memories we shared. Encountering a common object of little consequence to anyone else may serve as a message to us that a deceased loved one is sending a sign. The item triggers a memory and the story we shared with that person.

The use of color in devotional art is symbolic. We typically think of Mary wearing light blue, but artists clothed her in all the colors of the rainbow for a variety of reasons. In the sixth century, artists favored dark blue, the color of an empress. Later centuries often featured Mary in red, to indicate her royalty and suffering. The master artist, Raphael, dressed his Madonna in a red robe with a blue mantle. She also was draped in gold (for royalty) and black (for sorrow).

Sometimes Mary takes on a celestial appearance wearing a crown of stars and standing on the moon. This image is taken from the Book of Revelations. The verse reads, "A great portent appeared in the heaven: a woman clothed with the sun, with the moon under her feet, and on her head a crown of twelve stars" (12:1).

In recent centuries Mary is often portrayed more naturally. She is painted as described by visionaries who claim they received the blessing of seeing her apparitions, such as those from Medjugorje. Artists also depict Mary as the mother of all people, adapting her features to reflect those prominent in their own ethnicity. Portraits show her with native features, dress and surroundings. Artist Michael Walker painted Mary as the everyday Lady of Guadalupe. One example shows a Hispanic Mary wearing a crown while ironing her cloak. In the background hangs a family portrait of Joseph and Jesus.

Today's art incorporates a variety of mediums and every object imaginable. Computer art and photography are mixed with fine art. Some works are incredibly beautiful. Others are tacky or border disturbingly on the irreverent. Travel to any of the major pilgrimage sites and you find an assortment of souvenirs including drinking glasses, handbags and toys on which Mary's image is stamped. Of course rosaries, medals, paintings and statues of Mary made from wood, plaster, marble and plastic also are available.

౬ ౭

Sacred Icons

Icons are a specific type of fine art that date back to the Byzantine Empire. These works of devotion are as rich in history as they are in symbolism, incorporating Greek, Roman and Middle Eastern influences. Typically, these works are a one-dimensional portrait of a holy person. In the Orthodox faith, an iconostasis—a screen of icons—separates the sanctuary from the rest of the church. A miniature three-paneled variation of the iconostasis, which is often displayed in homes, is called a triptych.

Icons are believed to physically bring the viewer closer to the subject of the art. The icon is not the object of devotion, or confused as the subject, but it facilitates the connection between the viewer and the holy one represented. Those of the Orthodox faith believe that icons actually manifest the presence of the person represented, that the spirit who is depicted in the icon lingers where honor is shown to him or her. The faithful onlooker connects with Jesus, or the saint, by meditating on this powerful work of art.

Because of this connection, icons are considered sacred. Sometimes they are kissed and decorated with flowers. Votive candles may be lit beneath them to request a blessing or in thanksgiving for an answered prayer.

Icons are a very powerful prayer form because they begin in prayer and are specifically intended to promote prayer. The icon artist, called an iconographer or icon writer, prays throughout the process of this work. It is believed that divine guidance controls the human hand. Since God is the real artist, icons are not signed by the iconographer.

Icons of Mary frequently are created in request of assistance in diverting illness or disaster. Since the faithful believe Mary is present wherever the icon is displayed, the icon encourages her appearance and intercession. For this reason, believers visit these sacred works of art especially while grieving and in times of need.

The Orthodox faith identifies four major icons of Mary. The icons are recognized as the Mother of God Enthroned, the Mother of God Praying, the One Who Points the Way, and the Mother of God Merciful. There are many variations of these four types of icons including *Hodegetria*, The Greek Mother of God who leads the way, and *Eleosa*, the Compassionate Virgin.

Our Lady of Vladimir is another famous icon of Mary and the infant Jesus. Mary's face is long and sad and snuggled closely to her dear son. The painting is said to date to the twelfth century in Constantinople. It was taken from the city of Vladimir in 1155 and remains enshrined in the Cathedral of the Assumption in Moscow since 1395. The icon is displayed for protection in times of great celebration or distress.

౨ ౬

Mysterious Black Madonnas

Intrigue and awe surround the icons, paintings and sculptures depicting Mary with dark skin, known as black Madonnas. Legends tell of statues that are carved by heavenly hands and black Madonnas surviving devastating fires and vandalism. In general, black Madonnas are believed to offer protection to armies and cities from invasion and special graces and blessings to those who come in their presence to honor Mary.

When in need, pilgrims venture long distances to pray to Mary in areas where these pieces of art are found. They feel that being close to the artwork brings them closer to Mary and her blessings. This reassurance of her devotion to us, along with our devotion to her, results in great comfort and many answered prayers. Believers feel traveling to these particular types of artwork to be an essential step to take when suffering life's many traumas.

Some of the older Madonnas are recognized by the public as channels for miracles. Reproductions of them are considered just as powerful as originals. You will find the most well-known black Madonnas scattered throughout the world, from Our Lady of the Hermits in Einsiedeln, Switzerland, to Our Lady of Kazan in Russia, in addition to those in churches, shrines and private homes worldwide.

Black Madonna statues are typically about three feet high with varying degrees of artistic sophistication. In most, Mary is seated with the Christ child on her lap.

Both mother and son face forward. Often, Jesus' hand is raised in blessing and Mary is adorned with a crown.

Thrones of Wisdom are black Madonnas that contain compartments in the back or neck to hold relics. The Black Madonna of Chartres, France, holds what many believe is Mary's tunic. Another sculpture known as LePuy is alleged to carry her slippers.

Many of the black Madonnas were originally intended to be dark skinned. The artist most likely believed that Mary's skin tone was truly that shade, or the artwork was painted black in reference to the Hebrew interpretation of the Old Testament's Song of Song phrase, "black am I and beautiful." There also is some speculation that they were designed to replace the dark pagan goddesses displayed on pagan shrines. Other black Madonnas originally were light skinned but darkened over time due to paint oxidation, aging, and the accumulation of smoke and soot.

In previous centuries there was a public preference for dark virgins over light ones. When the black Madonna of Einsiedeln was taken from Switzerland to Austria in 1798 to protect it from invaders, the statue was cleaned and restored to its original light-skin tones. The restoration created such a surprising public outrage that it had to be repainted black.

☙ ❧

Our Lady of Czestochowa

A favorite legend surrounds the black Madonna referred to as Our Lady of Czestochowa, also known as Our Lady of Jasna Gora after the monastery in which it hangs in Czestochowa, Poland. The story begins with the evangelist St. Luke, who supposedly painted a portrait of the Virgin Mary and the child Jesus. The painting was made on three pieces of cedar wood from a table on which Mary ate. In the icon Mary's skin tone is dark and her features are elongated. She faces forward. Jesus' right hand is raised toward his mother's face; in his left hand he holds a box. Halos encircle both mother and child.

St. Helena, the Queen Mother of Emperor Constantine, found the portrait during a visit to the Holy Land in the fourth century. She brought it to Constantinople where it was then passed from one family to another in royal dowries. This practice demonstrates the icon's regard as a precious family heirloom. In the fifteenth century the portrait was presented to St. Ladislaus in Poland.

When the Tartars invaded Poland, St. Ladislaus wanted to protect the painting from vandalism, so he set out with it to the city of Opala. The journey took him through the town of Czestochowa where he stopped for the night. St. Ladislaus hung the icon in the Church of the Assumption on the hilltop of Jasna Gora for safekeeping while he slept. The next morning, he retrieved the painting and loaded it in his wagon, but no matter what he did, the horses refused to continue the journey. St. Ladislaus believed the icon was meant to remain in the little church and left it in Czestochowa.

Over the years the painting suffered damage on at least two occasions. At one time thieves stole it and broke the sacred art into three pieces. On another occasion, vandals slashed the Virgin's neck and right cheek. Ironically, restoration attempts were made to remove the marks, only for them to return.

Some analysts are convinced the icon is a reproduction. Original or not, the icon of Our Lady is no less treasured today than when it first arrived in Czestochowa. More than a million visitors travel each year to the shrine to honor the Virgin it represents and plea for her assistance. Whether grieving or suffering mental, physical or emotional anguish, they flock to this treasured black Madonna.

※ ※

Our Lady of Guadalupe

Love for Mary laid the common ground between people from differing cultures, time periods and faiths on more than one occasion. In general, love and sorrow binds us all. Our Lady of Guadalupe offers a case in point.

In the late sixth century Pope Gregory the Great gave a black Madonna statue to Archbishop Leandro of Seville, Spain. When the Arabs invaded the country in 711, the statue was buried in the mountains of Asturias along the Guadalupe River. (Burying sacred items was a common practice to prevent their desecration and theft.)

The legend is that five centuries later, Mary appeared to a man named Gil Codero and instructed him to dig for the buried sculpture. Codero retrieved the statue and placed it in a shrine on that same spot. The Spanish people showed honor to Our Lady of Guadalupe, Spain, by journeying to the shrine to pray.

Several centuries later, on December 9, 1531, across the ocean on the hills of Tepeyac, Mexico, a young peasant named Juan Diego was drawn to a bright light. There Juan found within a cloud a beautiful woman dressed in vivid colors. The woman spoke to him in his native Aztec tongue of Nahuatl. She said she was the Ever-Virgin, Holy Mary, Mother of the God of Truth. The Lady instructed Juan to go to Bishop Zumarraga of Mexico and tell him to build a chapel on the hill. However, it took Juan three attempts and a miracle before he convinced the bishop that this message indeed came from Mary.

In the midst of winter Mary provided what Juan thought was a sign for the bishop. It consisted of an exceptional bouquet of flowers, including Castilian roses, that he gathered from snow-covered hills per Mary's instructions. Mary arranged the flowers herself and wrapped them in Juan's own modest cloak, known as a *tilma*. However, it was a much more impressive sign than the beautiful flowers that Mary gave the bishop. Upon opening the cloak to present the bouquet, the exact image of Our Lady as revealed to Juan was printed on his *tilma*. The shocked bishop humbly dropped to his knees in tears.

The apparition was important to the indigenous people as well because it struck some significant correlations between the natives and their pagan gods:

- Mary was shown in bright, bold colors standing in the rays of the sun on a crescent moon. The indigenous people considered the goddess *Coatlicue* the mother of the sun and the moon.
- Mary told Juan that her name in his native tongue was *Tlecuauhtlacupeuh*, which means "the one who crushes the serpent." One of the native gods, *Quetzalcoatl*, was a feathered serpent to which people sacrificed women and children.
- The natives soon learned that while the serpent god required human sacrifice, Mary's son, Jesus, sacrificed himself for all people.

Not only did Mary speak to the people in their language, she reached out to Juan as his friend and protector. She told Juan not to let anything discourage or depress him. She said he should not fear any illness or pain, because she was his mother. She promised to protect him in the folds of her mantle in the crossing of her arms. After the apparitions millions were drawn to this special woman and her message, thereby converting to Christianity.

The Spaniards in Mexico were touched by the miracle

as well. *Tlecuauhtlacupeuh*, the name Mary used to address herself in the language of Nahuatl, sounded like the word "Guadalupe" to the Spaniards. The Lady even wore stars on her cloak as found on the ancient statue of Guadalupe, so the Spaniards believed she was their own Lady of their native land of Guadalupe, Spain.

In addition, Mary's relation with Juan forced the Spaniards to reconsider their perceptions of the indigenous people, whom they considered inferior. Mary honored the native culture with her presence. Consequently, the Spaniards had to recognize and respect them equally as children of God.

Scientists made several studies on the *tilma* to verify its authenticity. The scientific consensus consistently found that the icon truly is a heavenly creation. There are no brush strokes. Nor are the rich colors the result of any paint or dye known to humankind (with the exception of some flourishes added later).

The story of Our Lady of Guadalupe illustrates Mary's love for all people. However, she is most present to the poor, sad, sick and lonely because that is where she is most needed. She is with us in our grief and human pain. Mary's motherly concern is that everyone is treated justly and strives to live a life in a way that is pleasing to God. Her message always is to pray more and live peacefully.

Today, Juan's *tilma* is displayed in the world's busiest Marian shrine, Our Lady of Guadalupe Basilica, located in Mexico City. Millions of pilgrims travel worldwide each year to see the magnificent piece firsthand. From a moving walkway only a few feet below, pilgrims can see the image of Mary exactly as Juan saw her nearly five hundred years ago. The reality of the privileged opportunity to brush so closely to this self-portrait of our Blessed Mother is evident in the stream of awe-struck faces of the pilgrims beneath it. The experience is life-changing for the many people who claim they receive personal miracles in its presence.

After nearly five centuries, it is extraordinary that the *tilma* exists today unharmed and without deterioration of the cloth or colors. Made from the fibers of a cactus plant, it typically would disintegrate within twenty years. Also, a bomb exploded beneath it in 1921 ripping apart the marble in the sanctuary but without causing any damage to the *tilma* or its glass cover. The *tilma*'s incredible survival alone is an inspiration to patrons praying before it.

꙰ ꙱

Showing Your Devotion with Art

Mary is the epitome of human love and trust in God. She loved God so much that she wanted to do whatever God asked of her, no matter the risk or hardship. Her perfect faith and purity resulted in her being chosen to mother the Messiah. Only she was entrusted to carry and raise the most perfect human being.

We also may say that we submit to God's will, no matter how difficult a situation may be presented to us. In all honesty, that promise most often is made until we are faced with the challenge. Then we pray that God spares us any pain.

Gazing upon artworks of Mary is an important form of devotion because it can inspire us to live, love and trust as she did. The art reminds us that we are not alone. When we face the most trying and heart-wrenching episodes of our life, our Holy Mother is with us. She walks with us in our brightest and darkest days in the direction of her son.

Surround yourself with artwork created by any number of artists. Breathtaking portraits and sculptures may be viewed in museums, churches, books, and over the internet. Prints in all price ranges are available in many religious goods stores. Find one that is affordable and display it prominently in your home or office.

Creating your own art is another option. Showing devotion to Mary through art can be as creative as you are. Create an appliqué wall hanging or painting. If you are not artistic, make a collage of artwork gathered from magazines, books and the internet. Whatever you decide to work on, the process of making Marian art is your prayer, and designing each piece will be as meaningful to you as viewing it after completion. As all homemade gifts are gifts of oneself, you present a heartfelt gift of your time, talent and effort to our Blessed Mother.

Chapter Three

Basilica of Our Lady, Queen of the Holy Rosary.
Fatima, Portugal.

Devotion with Sacramentals

osaries turning gold-tone; paintings of Mary shedding tears of oil; Marian shrines emitting the fragrance of non-existent roses: These are some of the countless claims of extraordinary phenomena surrounding Marian sacramentals—religious articles associated with Mary. No proof is needed to convince witnesses of their validity. They know in their hearts that the odd occurrences truly happened. Mary personally touched them.

Having a Marian sacramental in your possession displays confidence in her assistance. Grasp a medal of Our Lady and you feel as if she is holding your hand. Wear a scapular and it is as if Our Holy Mother is embracing you. When life gets tough, there is no doubt that Mary is our partner on our pathway to God. She prays our prayers and walks through life with us.

Most Catholics have dozens of the sacramentals referred to as holy cards. Typically, they are four by two-and-a-half inches in size with a picture of Jesus, a saint or an angel on one side and a prayer on the other. There are hundreds of variations of cards of Mary specifying particular devotions, such as Our Mother of Perpetual

Help and Our Mother of Sorrows. Others highlight a prayer that honors her, such as the *Memorare* or the *Hail Mary*. Sometimes these devotional cards are given as a token gift or inserted in a greeting card.

One example has a picture of a young, sweet Mary on the front. Mary is wearing a light blue veil, simple white gown, and dark blue cloak, known as a mantle. She is touching her sacred heart with a delicate right hand. On the reverse side is the prayer to Our Lady of the Sacred Heart that begs for her protection and assistance in attaining a special request and declares trust in her intercession.

Catholic wakes usually present holy cards to guests paying their respects. The front of the cards may show any number of portraits of Jesus or Mary. A popular alternative today is to feature a photo of the deceased. A prayer and the loved one's name, date of birth and death, and place of burial are listed on the reverse side. The mementos give us something tangible to hold. Attendees save their cards in a Bible or keep them handy in their purse or wallet to serve as a reminder to pray for the souls of these people. Old Testament verses offer evidence that praying for the dead has been going on since ancient times. Scripture also encourages the giving of alms and works of penance on the dead's behalf (see 2 Maccabees 12:45).

Sacramentals, such as holy cards, are specific objects and actions instituted by the Church. They are intended to increase devotion and deflect evil. Sacramentals are constant reminders of God's ever presence and love for us and his gift of angels and saints to surround us. Through their use we pray that God bestows grace upon us and grants us mercy.

Only the Apostolic See—which is the diocese of Rome—determines the authenticity of an official sacramental change and can abolish or establish a new one. Most are reflective of Scripture. They often resemble the sacraments. For example, the sacramental of the blessing of throats on the feast of St. Blaise resembles the Sacrament of the Anointing of the Sick.

Other examples of sacramentals include holy water, holy oils, incense, candles and palms. Religious medals, crucifixes, Bibles and prayer books also are sacramentals. Some articles are specifically Marian, such as rosaries, icons and scapulars of Mary. Sacred places, such as the shrines in Lourdes, France, and Fatima, Portugal, also are considered Marian sacramentals.

Many actions are considered sacramental as well. These official liturgical rites of the church include genuflecting, making the sign of the cross, and blessings. Exorcisms, commissioning for various ministries, and the crowning of an image of the Blessed Virgin also are sacramental. Large or small, the actions are said to be transitory. This means that the sacramentality—the period of being sacramental—exists only while the action is taking place.

⚜ ⚜

Blessings

If a priest is leading a pilgrimage to a Marian shrine, he will bless the pilgrims before departing. This is a sign that the pilgrimage is being made in Mary's name to honor her and follow her lead. The pilgrims are blessed for taking on the responsibility to carry important prayers to Mary. Most often they return from the shrine with a desire to complete some work in Mary's name. It is as if they received an assignment they feel that Mary wants them to take on, such as an increased involvement with the sick and poor or teaching catechism classes.

The sacramental action of being blessed, especially when grieving, ill or troubled, is emotionally and spiritually healing. It is an acknowledgement that something extraordinary is occurring, that the people receiving the blessing are special in God's eyes. God loves them and is watching over them. They are able to let go of their worries and trust that God cares for them and the people they love.

Blessings are a sacred sign and expression of faith derived from the Word of God. The prayers and suggested Scripture readings for numerous blessings are found in the *Shorter Book of Blessings*. The blessings in this book are approved by the National Conference of Catholic Bishops for use in the United States. You will find blessings for people in a wide range of circumstances including pregnant women, the elderly, students, and victims of crime. The book also contains blessings for special occasions such as before an athletic event, fishing, places such as an office, or food.

The minister presiding over a blessing represents the Church, which is why most blessings are required to be conducted by a bishop or priest, or—if a priest is unavailable—a deacon, with the participation of the faithful. When no ordained is available, an acolyte, or reader formally instituted in that office in the Church, may conduct some blessings. A small amount of blessings, such as the blessing of children by their parents, may be celebrated by the laity, because every baptized person is called to be a blessing and to bless.

All blessings ultimately flow from God. Throughout the Hebrew and Christian Scriptures—the Old and New Testaments—we find references to blessings. People are blessed by the Lord and the Lord is blessed by the people. Jesus prayed a blessing before sharing a meal (see Mark 14:22) and tells us of those who are blessed (see Matthew 5:3-11, Luke 6:20-22). Elizabeth called Mary blessed (see Luke 1:42) and a woman in a crowd told Jesus that his mother's womb and her breast were blessed (see Luke 11:27).

Most Catholics own a number of blessed religious articles. The belief is that carrying a blessed sacramental serves as a guard against evil. It is a sign to the devil that we belong to God. The sacramental also serves as a reminder of God's love for us—to help us be more conscious and behave in a way that is pleasing to God. And when the sacramental is dedicated to Mary, it also serves as a request that she assist us with these goals.

※ ※

Marian Relics

Relics are special sacramentals because of their association with a holy person. The word relic comes from the Latin, *reliquias*, meaning "remains." Relics are divided into three classes:

1. The first group consists of parts of saint's bodies or instruments of Passion, such as fragments of Jesus' cross.
2. Objects which came in close contact to a saint's *living* body, such as clothing or personal items, belong to the second class.
3. Third order relics are ones that were touched to a holy person's *deceased* body.

We have evidence of extraordinary results from the use of relics since ancient times. Hebrew Scripture tells us of a man who came back to life after being buried in the grave of Elisha (see 2 Kings 13:20-21). From Scripture we also learn of healings that occurred when the sick were touched by cloths that came in contact with the Apostle Paul (see Acts 19:11-12). The belief is that contact with items that touched a holy person brings us closer to the saint who powerfully prays with us.

Mary's body was taken into heaven at the end of her life, so there are no first or third class relics of her. There were no remains of her body, no pieces of her bones. Nor could there be any items touched to her deceased body for third class relics, since no remains existed on this earth.

However, numerous European churches claim to possess an array of second class Marian relics. A cathedral in Asachem, Germany, built by Charlemagne has a cloth thought to have covered Mary's body at the end of her earthly life. This shroud is publicly displayed every seven years.

Several European churches state that they possess swatches of Mary's veil. The largest piece is contained in the Cathedral of Chartres, France. Constantine Porphyrogenitus and Irene gave this remnant of Mary's veil to Charlemagne. Charles the Bald then transferred it from Aachen to Chartres in about the year 876. The veil is encased in a golden reliquary except on the Feast of the Assumption, when it is carried through the streets.

The house in which it is said that Mary was born and where Jesus was conceived and raised also is considered a relic. Legend has it that this house was carried by angels in the 1290s from Nazareth to Loreto, Italy. The building is found today enclosed within a basilica built in 1728 by order of Pope Benedict XIII.

※ ※

Rosary Beads
Praying the rosary is one of the most beautiful ways to honor Mary and bring us closer to Jesus. When we

pray the rosary we meditate upon mysteries, the key moments in Jesus and Mary's lives. Contemplating on the mysteries, which includes the incarnation, ministry, crucifixion, resurrection and ascension of Jesus, helps to soften our hearts and become more Christ-like in our thoughts and actions.

The rosary is the greatest of all Marian sacramentals. It is believed that Mary promoted the rosary during several of her apparitions. Mary asked Blessed Bartolo Longo, Fortuna Agrelli and St. Bernadette to pray the rosary. She introduced herself to the shepherd children of Fatima as Our Lady of the Rosary and told them to pray the rosary every day.

Mary made several promises to those who pray the rosary faithfully. She said that we will obtain all we ask of her: special graces, protection against evil, and angels to assist us during life and at the hour of death. These are amazing assurances granted to us simply for spending time with her and Jesus each day. And these blessings extend to others when we pray the rosary for their intention.

Some of the most stressful times of life are periods of waiting. The unknown is often more frightening than the reality of a situation. Sacramentals, and the rosary in particular, are helpful in the minutes or hours spent waiting for medical test results, throughout legal battles and settlements, and even until a teen-aged child comes home late on a Saturday evening.

The rosary is effective in times of grief because its meditative effect is calming and reassuring. As with all forms of prayer, it is a source of comfort when little else is. Praying the rosary also helps us feel as if we are doing something constructive while occupying our hands and thoughts. If it is too difficult to concentrate on the entire rosary, praying three Hail Marys, as suggested in the Introduction, is a simple alternative. If that is not possible, sometimes just holding the rosary assures us that our heavenly mother is nearby—and also near the loved one we are worrying about.

Even if you have never used a rosary, you probably are familiar with this string of beads. Most people know of the traditional Dominican rosary with a crucifix, five beads, a centerpiece, and five sets of ten beads—known as decades—each separated by a single bead. Rosaries come in every color of the rainbow and are made from just about anything, most commonly seeds, wood, plastic, crystal, metals and semi-precious stones.

Praying the rosary basically consists of five prayers: the *Apostles' Creed*, *Our Father*, *Hail Mary*, *Glory Be*, and *Hail Holy Queen*, as well as meditation on one set of five mysteries, which are events in the lives of Jesus and Mary. The entire rosary actually consists of twenty decades with one bead between each decade. Other rosaries you may encounter are ladder rosaries, which have beads strung between two chains instead of on a single strand; lasso rosaries, which are sometimes given at weddings; Anglican rosaries; and Irish Penal Rosaries.

You also may find smaller versions of rosary beads called chaplets. Chaplets have a specific function. Their beads are set in symbolic patterns and colors. Some of the chaplets to Our Lady include the Chaplet of the Immaculate Conception, Seven Sorrows, and Seven Joys of the Blessed Virgin Mary. In the town of Medjugorje, Bosnia-Herzegovina, the common practice is to use a chaplet of seven sets of three beads on which an Our Father, Hail Mary, and a Glory Be is said daily before the traditional rosary.

The rosary is prayed every day all over the world. You probably are not surprised to hear that it is prayed in holy places like churches, shrines, convents and seminaries. But did you know that it is also prayed by some groups of brokers before the American Stock Exchange opens, construction workers, and police officers? Look closely when you are out and about. Rosaries are seen prayed on airplanes, hanging in cars from rearview mirrors, and on the walls of restaurants and medical facilities. In a troubled, turbulent world, the faithful are finding peace in praying the rosary in crowded public locations as well as in the privacy of their homes or church.

Many holy people are noted for their belief in the benefits of the rosary. Padre Pio, the stigmatic priest, called the rosary a weapon against evil. St. Louis de Montfort dedicated his life to promoting the rosary. His book, *The Secret of the Rosary,* is his testimony to its power. Pope

John XXIII spoke 38 times about Our Lady and the Rosary and prayed 15 decades daily. Pope John Paul II's devotion also is well known. He spoke openly and often about his devotion to Mary and the rosary as well.

If you wish to pray aloud with a community, call your local Catholic Church for times that rosary prayer groups are meeting. Praying with other people who are experienced with the rosary is very helpful in learning the order of the prayers and the mysteries. It is an enriching prayer experience to pray the rosary together. If your church does not have a designated time for rosary, call and suggest they start one. Or, maybe you want to lead a group yourself.

For further information on the rosary, read my book, *The Rosary Prayer by Prayer*. It offers a clear, easy way to pray the rosary. You only need to follow along page by page. In addition to historical information and extensive resources in the back of the book, you also will find Scripture verses, reflections, and original artwork for the mysteries to inspire your meditations.

❦ ❧

Medals

The custom of obtaining religious medals dates back to the age of catacombs. Medals retrieved from these underground burial chambers commemorate people, places and events. Many were designed as souvenirs for visitors wanting to remember their pilgrimage. The tokens offered a small way to carry home memories of an important trip.

There are nearly as many Marian medals as there are titles for Mary. You will find medals for Our Lady of Mount Carmel, Our Lady of Consolation, and Our Lady of Perpetual Help. In addition, shops surrounding famous Marian shrines such as Our Lady of Lourdes and Our Lady of Knock also sell their special medals.

Medals may be attached to anything from key chains to watches. Wearing a cross or medal around the neck is more than a fashion statement: It is an affirmation to the public of the wearer's personal beliefs. It also reassures the wearer that the object of the sacramental is close to their heart. When wearing a Marian medal, we are assured that Mary is with us.

The medal known as the Miraculous Medal is perhaps the most fascinating of all, not only because of the story of how the medal came about, but also for the stories that are told by those who wear it. The medal is rich in symbolism: Our Lady herself designed it. Mary showed the young novice, Catherine Laboure, in a chapel in the Sisters of Charity convent in Paris, France, exactly how she wanted it to look.

As with so many of the apparitions of Mary, the details of the vision are very significant:

• Mary stood on a snake on top of a globe and held a smaller globe in her hands. She said standing on the globe symbolized her queenship over heaven and earth.

- Mary opened her arms as light streamed from her fingers symbolizing the graces obtained by those who asked for them.
- Framing Mary was the inscription, "O Mary, conceived without sin, pray for us who have recourse to thee." The inscription was in reference to the authenticity of the dogma of the Immaculate Conception—an important topic of discussion at the time.
- When Mary turned around, twelve stars encircled a large "M" from which arose a cross. Below were two hearts in flames. One heart was encircled in thorns and the other was pierced by a sword. The twelve stars refer to the twelve apostles and the entire Church. There also is reference to the Book of Revelation (see 12:1) that states, "a great sign appeared in heaven, a woman clothed with the sun, and the moon under her feet, and on her head a crown of 12 stars." The cross symbolizes Jesus, the "M" is for Mary, and the two hearts are those of Jesus and Mary.

Mary instructed Catherine to strike a medal imprinted with these detailed images. She promised those who wore it, especially if they wore it around the neck, would receive great graces. The medal was approved by the Church and began production in 1832. Since then millions of medals have been distributed. Once referred to as the Our Lady of the Immaculate Conception medal, it now is known as the Miraculous Medal because of the number of people who claim to receive answers to their prayers while wearing it.

Scapulars

Wearing a scapular is the mark of a pledge of allegiance to Mary. With its use, we are asking our Holy Mother for her constant protection and assistance. Our Lady promised St. Simon Stock on July 16, 1251, that while wearing it the wearer thinks of her and, therefore, she thinks of the wearer. She also said that those who die while wearing a scapular will not suffer the fires of hell, because the devil is powerless in its presence.

The word "scapular" comes from the Latin, *scapulae*. Anyone can wear a scapular, but it is recommended that it is blessed and that the wearer be inducted into the confraternity of Scapular with a prayer. The sacramental consists of two small pieces of lamb's wool tied together with a ribbon or cord. It is worn around the neck with one piece of cloth in the front and one in the back.

The lamb's wool is symbolic of the Lamb of God. The swatch represents the monk's habit, which is made of wool. The original scapular is the brown scapular of Our Lady of Mount Carmel. Variations signify particular devotions including the:

- Green scapular of the Immaculate Heart of Mary
- White scapular of Our Lady of Good Counsel
- Blue scapular of the Immaculate Conception

- Black scapular of Seven Dolors of the Blessed Virgin Mary
- Scapular of the Sacred Hearts of Jesus and Mary
- Red Scapular of the Passion

Stories, legends and blessings abound in connection with the scapular. Many tell of the protection to people and property wearing or displaying it. According to the little booklet, *Garment of Grace*, published by the Immaculate Heart Publications, Blessed Pope Gregory X was buried wearing a scapular. When the tomb was opened 600 years after his death, the scapular had not disintegrated. And in 1957 in Westboden, Germany, twenty-two homes burned to ashes. The only house that remained had a scapular attached to the door.

Other stories tell how soldiers received protection in battle. One such incident involved a soldier who took off his scapular to wash himself. After he moved to another location with his battalion, he remembered leaving it behind. He hurried back to reclaim the scapular. When he returned to his battalion, he found that everyone else had been killed during his absence.

☙ ❧

Holy Water
Water is a vital element for all life forms. Our bodies consist mostly of water and need it for survival. Water also is symbolic of cleansing, purification and baptism.

Blessed water was sprinkled on early Christians as they entered the church. Use of such rituals helped instruct the predominantly illiterate congregation to remove the stain of their sins through prayer and confession before going to the Lord.

Scripture shows us examples of the use of water. The Lord told the Babylonian prophet, Ezekiel, that God would sprinkle clean water upon him and cleanse him of all impurities (see Ezekiel 37:25). Mary bathed herself for the rite of purification in accordance with the Law of Moses (see Luke 2:22). We also learn from Scripture that Jesus changed water into wine at the wedding in Cana (see John 2:3-10) and walked on water (see Matthew 14:25).

The healing quality of water, especially blessed water, is another facet of its importance. Water from sites of Marian apparitions including Knock, Ireland, Medjugorje, Bosnia-Herzegovina, and Fatima, Portugal, is collected in bottles of all sizes and carried home. Pilgrims believe it has miraculous qualities. There are numerous claims of answered prayers with its use.

The most famous Marian holy water comes from Lourdes, France. In 1858 it is believed that Mary appeared to a French girl named Bernadette Soubirous at the Grotto of Massabielle. Bernadette was searching for firewood when she met a beautiful young lady, who was later known to be Mary. Mary stood barefoot on two yellow roses. She was dressed in a white veil and robe with a blue sash. She held a rosary in her right hand.

Mary said that she was the Immaculate Conception. She asked for penance and prayer for the conversion of sinners. Mary also asked Bernadette to wash and drink from a spring near her feet. When Bernadette began to dig with her hands in the dry dirt, clear water trickled from the ground and developed into a spring that still exists today.

Since the apparitions, parades of pilgrims with mental, physical and emotional illnesses travel to the grotto to wash and drink from the extraordinary waters. Thousands of people attest to receiving personal miracles. The Church investigated and confirmed at least 65 of these cases.

❧ ❧

Praying with Sacramentals

The length of time needed to grieve after a loss or crisis is affected by many factors including the type of loss and preparation or anticipation of the event. Losing a financially and emotionally rewarding job leads to a different type of grief than the death of a loved one. The period of bereavement also is influenced by the existing support system. Loving friends and family, a supportive parish community, grief counselors, medical advisors, clergy, and other spiritual guides facilitate a healthy recovery and minimize physical, mental and emotional side effects. We learn by sharing our experiences that what we are feeling is normal and that the grieving will, at some point, diminish and finally end, or at least settle into a different, gentler form.

Prayer with sacramentals also can be helpful in the recovery process. During the most intense times of grief, concentration is difficult, and therefore so is prayer. A myriad of thoughts and feelings make clear thinking nearly impossible. Even the greatest saints found this to be so. Sacramentals may offer comfort in those times.

For this reason, devout Catholics often give gifts of sacramentals to grieving friends and family members. A blessed Miraculous Medal worn close to your heart, a rosary in your pocket, and the sense of cleansing from blessing oneself with holy water, especially water from a Marian shrine, is very healing. The sacramentals are not magic tokens or amulets but do promote the reminder that Mary is with us. Our loving, heavenly mother hears our prayers in our sadness as well as our joy.

Chapter Four

Maria Lanakila Church.
Lahaina, Maui, Hawaii.

Devotion in Motion

From lighting a candle to walking miles on a pilgrimage, "devotion in motion" can take on many forms. Some practices are more obviously pious, but opening a door for a stranger, spoon-feeding the sick, and sending "thinking of you" notes to the lonely are at least as prayerful as getting down on your knees or blessing yourself with holy water. All are ways to move our prayers from our hands to God's.

Devotion in motion not only expresses our innermost prayers in a physical way, it heals on several levels. First, spiritual benefits result from all forms of prayer. In our deliberate attempt to communicate with God, we build our relationship with and become closer to God. The desire and ability to be more God-like is increased.

Activity also provides the opportunity to voice our concerns. We must ask for what we want. This may be done confidently because Jesus said, "So I say to you, ask, and it will be given to you; search, and you will find; knock, and the door will be opened for you. For everyone who asks receives, and everyone who searches finds, and for everyone who knocks, the door will be opened" (Luke 11:9-10). When we call on Mary to pray with us, she joins us in asking, searching and knocking.

From a purely physical standpoint, devotion in motion helps strengthen our bodies. The more vigorous the action, the more benefits result. Activities such as climbing the mountains at the pilgrimage site in Medjugorje, Bosnia-Herzegovina, can burn quite a few calories. In addition, as with all physical exercise, endorphins are released—relieving stress and making prayer with movement a healthy option for mind, body and spirit.

Devotion in motion promotes emotional healing as well, because it helps us feel proactive. We are doing something constructive and not just waiting for a response. The movements keep us busy in the interim between asking for and receiving an answer. We feel that we are participating in our recovery by literally taking steps toward our problem's resolution.

The outward expression of prayer by others is inspiring. Witnessing people intensely praying stirs our own level of devotion. It is very moving to see a line of people crawling on their knees to a Marian shrine or to participate in praying the rosary with hundreds of others in a packed church. The love and faith of those surrounding us deepen our own hope and trust that our prayers are important to Mary and Jesus and that they are being heard.

In addition, when we pray in the company of others, our prayers become their prayers, adding significantly to the power of our supplication. Jesus said praying together was very effective. He said, "Again, truly I tell you, if two of you agree on earth about anything you ask, it will be done for you by my Father in heaven. For where two or three are gathered in my name, I am there among them" (Matthew 18:19-20).

※ ※

Taking Action for Mary

Traditional devotional actions are particularly easy to do because they are comfortable movements we have practiced since childhood. We don't need to put much thought into them. Even when under tremendous stress, walking into a church and praying before a holy image comes easily and naturally for Catholics with a history of doing so. Afterwards, most faithful people attain a sense of relief. Their personal grief is lighter after releasing it from their control.

Many of these sacred motions are Marian in nature. But it is important to remember that when we pray to Mary, in actuality we are praying *with* her. Our prayers do not end with Mary but continue through her. We are asking her to pray our intentions and take them to her son. It is Jesus and the Father to whom we ultimately bring our concerns.

Publicly-displayed statues and paintings of Mary typically have candles before them. Followers of Mary appreciate the opportunity to approach her from such a place. The ritual of lighting candles is rich in symbolism. Striking a match, lighting the wick, blowing out the match, and watching the dancing flame and ensuing smoke represents gathering our prayers and sending them up to the heavens. Due to fire and safety laws, many churches replace the candles with votive light bulbs. Pressing a button might not have the same resonance, but the symbolism and results remain the same.

There are at least dozens, perhaps hundreds, of organizations that make a practice of performing Marian devotions. These communities are dedicated to promoting deeper devotion to Jesus following the model of Mary. Each has a slightly different and special intention and method of devotion.

For example, some are devoted to the promotion and practice of praying the rosary. Others distribute literature and supplementary forms of information on Mary or an aspect of her, such as the Queen of the Americas Guild, which raises awareness about the miracle of and devotion to Our Lady of Guadalupe. These groups sponsor conferences, retreats, social service programs, and publications that teach and evangelize. A few examples include the Association of the Miraculous Medal, Cenacle of our Lady of Divine Providence, and Our Lady's Rosary Makers, to name a few.

It isn't difficult to find one that is best for you to participate with. The Association of Marian Helpers, founded in 1944, is an organization that produces and distributes Catholic literature and promotes the role of

Mary. The Family Rosary was founded in 1942 after the founder recovered from tuberculosis. Its intention is to increase family prayer, especially the rosary. The well-known Legion of Mary, founded in Ireland by Frank Duff in 1921, strives to give glory to God through prayer and cooperation in Mary's and the church's work of advancing the reign of Christ. And the Madonna's Center is a nonprofit group that addresses the concerns of teen pregnancy.

⚜ ⚜

Laying on of Hands

We shake hands with strangers, pat a coworker on the back for a job well-done and greet loved ones with a kiss. Human contact is vital to emotional survival. Studies show that babies fail to thrive physically and emotionally if they are not cuddled. It's also proven that many physical ailments are greatly improved with rehabilitation and massage therapy. People recover quicker and more fully from illness and trauma with a little tender loving care.

When we are sad or frightened, friends and caretakers naturally shower us with hugs. The healing effect of the simple gesture is amazing and very important to most people recovering from grief. The hug is a physical sign of support, one person to another. It tells us that we do not have to endure the suffering alone. There are other people who will help us carry the load.

Along this line of thought, a special type of blessing uses hands. It is referred to as the laying on of hands, also known as the imposition of hands. Laying on of hands is a powerful instrument in healing. It also is very humbling, very moving.

Most likely you have seen this practiced at least on one occasion at Mass. Many priests will ask for the community's participation in a blessing of parishioners engaged in a special project, situation or celebration. When the congregation reaches out together, we see a visible sign of support. We feel the energy of a community acting with one loving intention.

Laying on of hands has ancient roots. Evidence of this practice is found in both Testaments. It is a basic teaching about Christ (see Hebrews 6:2). The Lord told Moses to lay his hand upon Joshua (see Numbers 27:18); and Jesus was asked to lay his hand on the daughter of a synagogue leader who died (see Matthew 9:18-19). The apostles followed Jesus' example by utilizing the imposition of hands (see Acts 6:6, 8:17, 13:3, 19:6).

If you have the opportunity to participate in such a ceremony, please do. You will find it healing whether you are extending the gift of your love and support through your hands or receiving this blessing from the other members of the community. Either way, the practice connects us, brothers and sisters, to one another—all children of one Almighty God.

✻ ✻

Labyrinths

Walking a labyrinth is a meditative and healing experience that helps relieve stress, at least temporarily, by quieting the mind. Like a voyage to the center of our being, walkers claim that it promotes a sense of peace, compassion and understanding. The special walk offers a period of repose, a peaceful break from life's challenges. It assists with releasing anger, pain and ego and ends with a feeling of hope, insight and serenity, all of which are important and necessary aspects of healthy grief recovery.

Labyrinths are pathways consisting of one continuous, circular route in and out of a hub. There are no dead ends or split paths as found in mazes. The path may consist of three to eleven circuits, and contain shapes of crosses, stars, polygons, roses or knots. The most common design has a circular pattern with eleven concentric circles surrounding a rosette center. There is one single path which leads in and out. The path weaves back and forth around sections of the circle.

Labyrinths may be marked on the ground with paint or stonework, woven in tapestry, or even stamped on a tarp. Some are edged with materials such as shrubbery, candles, paper or wood. Most are large enough to physically walk, extending to six hundred feet or more in size. Others are very small and intended to be traced with your fingers.

Many lessons are learned from the labyrinth. Like life,

the distance from our goal can be deceptive. Often when the path leads closer to the center, the walker actually is a long distance away. Other times when the walker is moving along the outermost walkway, they actually are nearing the center.

This trail emphasizes that, no matter how far away we feel from answered prayers, in time, our prayers always are answered. We may not recognize the answer because it isn't exactly what we wanted or how we thought the outcome would look. However, we must trust that the response is in the best interest of our whole life's journey.

Labyrinths are found in cathedrals, retreat centers, hospitals, and public gardens. They also are in some airports and on the Internet. Perhaps most well-known is the thirteenth-century labyrinth in the Chartres Cathedral in France. Many constructed in the United States, such as the one in Episcopal Grace Cathedral in San Francisco, California, are replicas of the labyrinth at Chartres.

The first labyrinth was built in Egypt around 1800 BC—four thousand years ago. Other remains of ancient labyrinths were found in Sardinia, Crete, Syria and Greece. Although the early civilizations of these countries were distant from one another, they designed and developed similar concepts of labyrinths.

Labyrinths are rich in symbolism. They are constructed in connection with many churches because they represent the pathway of life and the journey to salvation. Also, many theories exist as to the meaning of the petal-shaped center. The six inner petals may represent the six days of creation or the six different kingdoms of mineral, plant, animal, human, angelic and the divine. The center also is thought to represent the Holy Spirit or the cycles of the moon.

Some labyrinths are believed to contain Marian symbolism as well, and are therefore dedicated to our Holy Mother. The rosette center in particular correlates with the symbolism of roses that is typically associated with Mary. Churches and organizations all over the world hold special events to honor Mary in association with walking labyrinths. Chartres Cathedral has many such events.

The devotion in motion of walking a labyrinth may be used to honor a birthday, anniversary, graduation or other benchmark. You also might walk it in honor of a deceased friend or relative. At one time, pilgrims walked or crawled labyrinths as an act of penance. Mostly, people use the pathway to ease a situation weighing heavy on their heart. By putting one foot in front of the other, they take steps to resolve stressful situations by asking for assistance or meditating on possible solutions. The overall result is a tremendous sense of calm, which is particularly welcome while grieving.

There are no rules for walking the labyrinth. The process depends on your current concerns and mood. Most walkers begin by taking a moment to pause at the entrance. At that time, or throughout the walk, a question may be presented, a mantra repeated, or a prayer said. Focus is placed on a particular image or thought, or the mind may remain open.

At one time, the labyrinth was called the Threefold Path. It was walked to achieve a better relationship with God. Purgation is the first stage and the portion of the labyrinth from the entrance to the center. With each step during this segment, what lays heavy on the heart is released.

Walkers often feel a sense of joy and relief upon reaching the center, the second stage of Illumination. It is a place of calm, meditation and prayer. Here, a new understanding, a sense of clarity, or an answer often is realized. It is good to stop in the center for a few minutes to enjoy the sensation.

The path out from the center is the third stage of Union. This section is symbolic of our union with God and reunion or communion with the rest of the world. Walkers leave the labyrinth and return to their daily life replenished. Often they have a new or stronger insight to their life purpose.

゛゛

Feasts and Processions

For those devoted to Mary, every occasion is an opportunity to show her how much she is loved and how much we need her to support us in good times and bad. She is especially honored in the month of May. Some schools and churches conduct May Crownings where Marian hymns are sung and a statue of Mary is crowned with a wreath of flowers. She's also remembered at weddings by brides who wish to imitate her love for Jesus. The tradition is for the bride to bring flowers to a statue or painting of Mary and ask her to bless the marriage.

The Church celebrates a number of Feast Days in Mary's honor that are categorized by their level of importance. The highest-ranking category is solemnities. These are the days when Catholics are required to participate in Mass, although the number of days differs by country. The U.S. solemnities include the Solemnity of Mary, Mother of God (Jan. 1); Annunciation (Mar. 25); Immaculate Heart of Mary (Saturday following Second Sunday after Pentecost); Assumption (Aug. 15); and Immaculate Conception (Dec. 8).

The second category is officially called "Feast Days." These days are of significance but do not include an obligation to attend Mass. The Marian Feast Days are the Presentation of the Lord (Feb. 2), Visitation (May 31), Dedication of Saint Mary Major (Aug. 5), Birth of Mary (Sep. 8), and Our Lady of Guadalupe (Dec. 12).

Memorials are the lowest-ranking group and are subcategorized as obligatory or optional. Obligatory memorials must be celebrated in the liturgical calendar but are not considered a Holy Day of Obligation, whereas optional days are to be celebrated at the discretion of the priest celebrant. The Marian memorials are Our Lady of Lourdes (Feb. 11); Our Lady of Mount Carmel (July 16); Queenship of Mary (Aug. 22); Our Lady of Sorrows (Sep. 15); Our Lady of the Rosary (Oct. 7); and the Presentation of Mary (Nov. 21).

The oldest Marian feast day in the church calendar is a combination of the Assumption, which was previously known as the Dormition, and Mary's recognition as the *Theotokos*, the God-bearer. This feast began in the Eastern Church around 450 and in the Roman rite sometime in the sixth or seventh century. Early Christians believed Mary's role as Mother of God and her Assumption to be the most important aspects of her, the reasons for which she is due our utmost respect.

Mary is remembered in the liturgy for her participation in the mystery of Christ and for her role in the history of salvation. She is recognized in the Nicene Creed and with some of the Eucharistic prayers. In addition, the National Conference of Catholic Bishops in the United States approved a number of Marian feast days. Feast Days offer important opportunities to ask Mary for assistance. So many answered prayers are claimed to be received on these days that it must please her to see people coming together in her honor to pray to her son. It is as if our Holy Mother rewards her children by taking our worries and fears from us when we make the effort and show our faith in approaching her.

Communities all over the world claim a particular
Marian feast day or assign her a title of special interest.
They commemorate their heavenly mother with prayer,
music, food and friendship. Devotees express their love
for Mary in ways that are unique to their culture. Festivals may include marching bands, fine dress, fireworks,
candles, flowers and native dances. Statues or portraits
of Mary are sometimes adorned with jewels and robed
in lace or ornately-embroidered fabrics.

In the Hispanic community, a tradition is to burn pil-
lar candles in decorative glass domes before Marian images. Often the glass is printed with the image of Our
Lady of Guadalupe. Whether their prayers are for good
health or abundant harvest, the people trust Mary to
present their requests to her son. Their faith is strong in
her intercession.

Mary is remembered as the Mother of Mercy at the
Shrine of the Gates of Dawn in the walls of the old city
of Vilnius, Lithuania. Praying the rosary is an important
show of devotion in this community. During World War
II civilians showed their rosaries to German forces when
they were asked for their identity papers. Lithuanians
pray to Mary, the Mother of God, with confidence in
her love, mercy and compassion.

In Spain, traditions honoring *La Virgen*, called *Rome-
rias*, are practiced yearly at festivals in each town. Thousands of people attend. In Toledo, the people spend the
night before the feast day camping in the mountains

close to the church where the statue of the Virgin is displayed. In the South of Spain, the *Virgen Rocio* is celebrated. A statue of Mary is carried through the streets. The crowd sings Marian flamenco-type songs, known as *saetas*, and waves to the procession from their balconies or from places along the street.

The feminine energy runs strong through "Mama Africa," as the country is often referred to by Africans, prompting reverence for Mary (particularly in Nigeria). This devotion took root in the large Islamic, as well Christian, community, when the Irish missionaries came to spread the Word of God. Evidence of this is found in the Blue Army, an international movement that responds to the requests of the Blessed Virgin Mary at Fatima. The devotion of African Christians is quite joyful. In addition to regular recitation of the rosary and Litany of Mary, Africans undertake long journeys on steamy busses to Marian shrines. Throughout the pilgrimages, the atmosphere is festive as Marian hymns come alive with passionate singing and drumming.

When these ethnic groups transplant to other countries, they bring their cultural and religious practices to their new lands. Communities in North America replicate the traditions and devotions of their homeland, often with an American twist. Prayer intertwines with colorful festivities for the celebration of the Mother of all the people. These occasions are important opportunities for people to place their worries and concerns before Mary and honor her in personally meaningful ways.

⚜ ⚜

To Mary through Sacrifice

Mother Teresa of Calcutta called suffering the "kiss of Jesus." She said that those who struggle are particularly blessed. Their pain is a sign that they are close enough to Jesus to be kissed by him.

Mother Teresa said that the crucifix indicates God's desire to love us. If you look at the cross you will see that Jesus' head is bent down so that he can kiss you. His arms are open to embrace you. His heart is open to receive you.

We all can keep this beautiful perception in mind, because people from every walk of life experience hardships. For some it is a daily struggle for survival, people barely getting by, worrying over the ability to provide food and shelter for their families. Many other people live in chronic pain or deal with the changes and difficulties resulting from illness and aging or the loss of a job, pet, friend or relative. There also are numerous areas in the world that suffer from conflict, terrorism and civil unrest.

In ancient times, suffering had a stigma attached to it. Many believed that those who were disadvantaged or ill were in that condition because of their imperfect relationship with God. The sufferer must have angered the Lord, and therefore deserved their predicament. The general public avoided contact with them for fear that in their presence God would punish them as well.

We have since come to understand that this is not so. Jesus in his human person was absolutely pure and sinless, yet he suffered greatly. Bad things do happen to good people. The Lord's reason for our suffering is unknown to us.

God allows humans to act on their own free will. Good people are victims of bad situations because of the prevalence of human failings and weaknesses in the world at large. Sin contaminates the whole of humanity, affecting those not responsible for the sin as well as those who are.

Perhaps people suffer in order to present an opportunity for others to care for them and be Christ-like. And through our suffering, we experience spiritual growth and grace. It is a means of participating in the suffering of Christ. Saint Paul wrote to the Roman community that this is the mark of the true Christian. He said, "Rejoice in hope, be patient in suffering, persevere in prayer" (Romans 12:12).

Suffering can serve a purpose. It assists with the struggle to abandon ego. It is an opportunity to build character, teach lessons, and increase our empathy for others who suffer, granting symbolic expression to humanity's submission to God. Many people who are enduring their own painful situations offer their anguish to Jesus, and sometimes Mary, as a gift or compromise.

At times, suffering is intentionally self-inflicted. Kneeling or walking on the knees to a prayerful destination is one example. Such actions are offered as penance or a show of surrender. They promote hope in God's love and mercy.

Fasting is a deliberate action practiced in many religions to assume a sense of suffering. For Christians it is an imitation of Christ and his suffering on the cross. Moses (see Exodus 34:28) and Jesus (see Matthew 4:2) both fasted for forty days. Jesus did not need forgiveness, but by fasting he showed us how we may approach the Lord. Our fasting is an expression of sorrow for the ways in which we fail to honor God. It symbolizes our acceptance of the responsibility we take for the sins of humanity. It is a form of doing penance for the forgiveness of sin and an effort to reconcile with God.

Jesus said that he is the bread of life. If we go to him we will never be hungry (see John 6:35). Fasting is a sign that we believe this to be true. Jesus is the only nourishment that we need.

The visionaries of the Marian apparitions in Medjugorje claim that Mary says there are several practices that are imperative for our spiritual health, one of which is fasting. They say that Mary also urges us to pray the rosary, receive the Eucharist, seek monthly confession, and read the Bible daily. Mary's intention always is to bring us closer to Jesus. When we honor her by following her instructions, we move closer to the goal of improving our relationship with her son.

🙠 🙡

Moving with Mary

Mary is both the object and partner of Marian devotion in motion. We physically go *to* Mary and ask her to go *with* us to God. As illustrated, there are countless ways to do this. Some of the activities are easily recognized as spiritual, such as reading the Bible or kneeling in prayer. Others are more subtle, such as serving in a homeless shelter or offering up our own pain.

In periods of bereavement, these types of actions are very consoling. When the mind is distracted with heartache, physical expressions of devotion are a good alternative. Our time and energy are used in a positive way until we are able to perform our regular prayer more easily. We walk the labyrinth with Mary and together send our prayers to the Lord.

Chapter Five

Our Lady's Shrine.
Knock, County Mayo, Ireland.

Devotion in Sacred Spaces

A hospital chapel, majestic basilica, or backyard Mary garden: Sacred spaces offer a place of peace and prayer. The setting can be anywhere. All one needs is a quiet spot to meditate, read the Bible, listen to music, or sit in silence. When we are troubled, these areas give us a place to be alone with God. They are little clouds of heaven on earth.

For thousands of years, pilgrims have traveled to holy places, often at great personal sacrifice. They attend festivals, meet religious obligation, gather with members of a faith community, pray, and relax. More so, they go to seek healing, reconciliation with God, answers to prayers, and to walk in the footsteps of holy people before them. Sometimes, their greatest desire is for a miracle. The pilgrims venture to these locations with great hope in God's love and mercy. They believe God will appreciate their sacrifices and fulfill their request, even if their request seems impossible.

Many of these pilgrimage sites are dedicated to Mary. They are intended to honor her and promote her messages of prayer, the importance of reading the Bible, and conversion. Pilgrims also pray that Mary will pray with them. Together with Mary, pilgrims take their prayers to Jesus. The second Vatican council document, the Dogmatic Constitution on the Church, *Lumen Gentium*, states that Jesus is the only mediator. We do not need Mary to mediate for us. What we ask, however, is that she helps us bring our worries to her son.

Pilgrims venture to Marian shrines worldwide. Each site has a different feel. Some are peaceful, lovely places with lush gardens, such as the sanctuary of Knock, Ireland. Others are very busy with the movement of millions of people, such as the one in Lourdes, France. Which is best for you depends on your personal style of prayer, intention and budget.

The major Marian shrines are sites of known apparitions—appearances of Mary's holy presence. Smaller, intimate shrines are found within driving distance of most of our homes. Although not recognized sites of apparitions, they are special, out-of-the-way places where we are able to concentrate on a conversation with our heavenly mother. We can gather our troubles and present them to her without distraction.

❧ ❧

Apparitions

Most devout people experience an occasion of heightened awareness of God's presence. Not only do they see God's imprint on all that is good, they have enjoyed at least one occasion when they knew God walked with them, guided them, or allowed a complicated situation to resolve ever so peacefully and easily. However, even the holiest people are not guaranteed the extraordinary gift of an apparition—an unexplainable appearance of beings that do not physically live on this earth, such as Jesus, Mary, angels or saints. Apparitions occur when, and if, heavenly beings desire. We cannot make them appear to us.

It is important to remember that, in our struggles and heartaches, we are never alone. God always is present to us in Scripture, the sacraments, and the life around us. God's goodness, mercy and generosity are evident in the people, experiences and wonders of our daily lives. In addition, God surrounds us with saints and angels to guide and protect us, whether or not we see them.

Mary is one of those heavenly beings. She is with us, and an astonishing number of people believe they have seen or heard her or sensed that she was physically close to them. This includes ordinary people from differing income levels, ages and nationalities. Children and teens, men and women, wealthy and poor, scholarly and uneducated people are aware that, especially in times of sorrow, our heavenly mother is nearby. Mary shows herself to those whom she feels need her, and she comes to deliver messages that need to be heard.

People who have encountered Mary understand the event is a private gift, relevant only to them. When pressed, their stories are told in a humble whisper. They become emotional even decades afterwards. For many, the experience was life-changing, projecting them in a new and holier direction.

Other apparitions are thought to carry an important message for an entire community. The witnesses then are encouraged to present their case before the Church. However, the Catholic Church is very cautious with her investigation of apparitions. There must be nothing in the account contrary to Scripture or the teachings of the Church; nor can the apparition be explained by an impediment in the visionary's mental health or character or by natural phenomenon. Also, there cannot be any trace of fraud or evil. The end result should promote an increased faith and some miraculous physical, emotional or spiritual change in believers.

Investigative consideration is given to the accuracy of the visionary as a reporter. Adults tend to interpret and repeat things from their own perspective and understanding, which slightly alters the meaning. Details may be lacking or incorrect. Even a well-intentioned and honest seer may unconsciously taint a message or omit important details.

Most of the approved apparitions occurred in the presence of children. This may be because of their innocence and purity. Children have no personal agenda or prejudice to interfere with their reporting. Often, they do not even understand the message. The vocabulary is beyond their comprehension. Therefore, they are most likely to repeat Mary's words verbatim.

The Church also weighs the intent of an apparition. Its publication must have a clear purpose. The message should promote Biblical teachings and not contradict or add to the gospel. Ultimately, all aspects of the apparition are required to build on our relationship with God. When Mary does appear to us, she does so only for the purpose of promoting the Trinity: God the Father; her son, Jesus; and the Holy Spirit.

The apparitions witnessed by the shepherd children in Fatima, Portugal, offer a case in point. In one of the apparitions Mary promised a sign to anyone who came to pray together in the field on October 13, 1917. Few of the crowd of 70,000 saw the apparition of Mary on that promised day, but most did acknowledge what is known as the Miracle of the Sun. At that time witnesses said the sun appeared to fall, spin and spray a succession of colored rays over the people. Many also claimed immediate, personal miracles.

Although the Church quickly determined the six months of Marian apparitions that proceeded the Miracle of the Sun to be worthy of belief, it did not see a benefit in investigating the portion of it that included the bizarre astrological occurrences. The Church stated that it was too difficult to determine the origin of that phenomenon, even though most found it to be spiritually moving. More so, the approval of the spinning sun had little benefit to the general community. It did not add to her primary message: Keep Jesus first in our lives.

Actually, the Church does not require the faithful to believe any part of an approved apparition. The most positive ruling that can be awarded a case is that it is worthy of belief (nothing about it is contrary to the faith). However, if the determination is that the case is contrary to belief, or if the Church finds some aspect of the apparition false, we are forbidden to believe.

The Church has investigated the authenticity of Marian apparitions since at least the third century. The last two hundred years are sometimes referred to as the Marian Age because of the frequency of sightings. Nearly four hundred cases of Marian apparitions were brought before the Church for rulings in the twentieth century alone. The Church found some of these claims not contrary to the faith—meaning that although they did not contradict the basic truths of our faith, the case also was not necessarily worthy of belief. To date, only a handful of alleged Marian sightings have been determined positively worthy of belief.

Still, the list of countries where people maintain that Mary appeared is impressive. Our Lady of the Universe reaches out to all of her children, over and over again.

Visionaries alleging to have received an apparition of
Mary live in countries including:

- Africa
- Algeria
- Argentina
- Australia
- Belgium
- Bosnia-
  Herzegovina
- Brazil
- Burundi
- Cameroon
- Canada
- Chili
- China
- Columbia
- Czech
  Republic
- Ecuador
- Egypt
- France
- Germany
- Great Britain
- Greece
- Haiti
- Holland
- Hungary
- Iraq
- Ireland
- Italy
- Japan
- Korea
- Lebanon
- Lithuania
- Luxembourg
- Mexico
- Mozambique
- Nicaragua
- Nigeria
- Philippines
- Poland
- Puerto Rico
- Portugal
- Romania
- Russia
- Rwanda
- Slovakia
- Slovenia
- Spain
- South Africa
- Switzerland
- Syria
- Taiwan
- Ukraine
- United States
- Venezuela
- Vietnam
- Yugoslavia
- Zaire

The extent of Mary's visits indicates a pressing need
for us to turn away from sin and work toward a greater
union with Jesus. Mary is often said to request an increase
in prayer and repentance. Her greatest intention is that
we, her children, continuously move closer to Jesus. She
desperately wants us to keep her son first in our lives.

And Mary's pleas are urgent. Few would deny that we live in an age of spiritual warfare. The sacredness of the priesthood and marriage are under attack. Drug and alcohol addiction, abortion, child and spousal abuse, over-consumption of consumer goods, and irreverence toward our planet dominate the evening news.

Due to the condition of the world, some of Mary's messages carry a warning. For example, when Mary appeared to the three shepherd children of Fatima, she said she was the Lady of the Rosary and asked the children to pray the rosary every day to obtain world peace. (This practice encourages meditation on the fundamental beliefs of our Christian faith and greater communication with God.) Mary warned that if people did not increase the frequency of their prayers and move closer to God, the world was at risk of a worse war than what they were currently experiencing (World War I).

The people of Portugal took Mary's words seriously and made a massive conversion. The world at large did not. The result, as we know, was the development of the Second World War and the loss of millions of lives. Some believe God spared Portugal from involvement in that war because of their prayers.

※ ※

Seeking Miracles

The major Marian shrines are on sites where there are church approved or recognized claims of Marian apparitions. People venture from across the globe to these locations to be closer to earthly places where Mary graced us with her heavenly presence. Believers seek comfort for those who struggle, suffer and grieve.

These sanctuaries offer both public and private areas to pray. Most are set in the midst of picturesque landscaping, statues, confessionals, adoration chapels, and churches with ongoing Masses, prayer services, and devotional candles. More so, all such sites spark a remarkable number of testimonies of unexplained medical healings, conversions and other miracles.

These shrines are heavenly gifts. They offer us destinations where we can establish a closer connection with God. We also can find a concentration of faithful people in prayer. Believers gather together, inspiring and elevating each of our levels of faith.

Through our prayers and visits to holy places, miracles may result. Saint Paul said that God gives some people the gift of miracles activated by the Holy Spirit (see 1 Corinthians 12:4-11). Undoubtedly, pilgrims believe this to be true. This is evident in the number of people who go to Marian sites each year seeking their own special miracles. Millions of people believe Mary will assist with their heartaches.

Yet caution must be taken. The goal of a pilgrimage should be not only to bring our sorrow and pain to the Lord but most of all to appreciate the opportunity to deepen our relationship with Christ. We then may trust that, when we seek Jesus, miracles happen. God is surely capable of unlimited blessings. The faith is in accepting that God heals in God's own way.

Healing waters are a prominent aspect of holy sites because of their perceived miraculous component. Pilgrims collect water from streams that sprang upon Mary's visit or sources near where she appeared. Such water is believed to be blessed by her, and therefore, particularly therapeutic. The healing can be emotional, physical or spiritual, all of which contribute toward better overall well-being.

Unexplained occurrences that glorify God, known as miracles, are told throughout the Hebrew and Christian Scriptures. Those which occur with the intercession of a saint, such as Mary, prove the saint's powerful relationship with God. But once again, it is important to remember that all miracles are gifts from *God*, not the saint who prayed with us.

In declaring a medical physical cure from waters or a visit to a shrine, a thorough and extensive medical examination is required. First, the illness must be diagnosed prior to the miracle. Second, medical professionals must determine the prognosis to be permanent or terminal. This means that there is no known cure for the disability or illness. Lastly, the cure has to occur immediately (without convalescence), completely and lastingly. No previously-prescribed treatment can be attributed to the cause of the cure or aided by it.

꽃 ꩜

Marian Shrines

Six young people in Medjugorje, Bosnia-Herzegovina, have claimed ongoing Marian apparitions since the early 1980s. The apparitions occurred daily for many years for all of the visionaries. As of 2009 three of them—Vicka Ivankovic-Mijatovic, Marija Pavlovic-Lunetti, and Ivan Dragicevic—continue to receive daily apparitions. Ivanka Ivankovic-Elezand and Jakov Colo receive one apparition each year. Mirjana Dragicevic-Soldo continues to receive an apparition each year on her birthday and a verbal message on the second of each month.

The Medjugorje visionaries say that Mary's messages focus on the need for peace in the world. Mary tells them that peace is obtained through communication with God, faith and trust in the Lord, and conversion. She says that prayer, reading Scripture, fasting on bread and water twice a week, and frequently receiving the Eucharist is imperative. Mary is quoted as saying, "I have come to tell the world that God exists. He is the fullness of life, and to enjoy this fullness and peace you must return to God."

Although Medjugorje is a popular destination for pilgrimages, the ongoing apparitions to the Medjugorje visionaries are not officially recognized by the Church, nor can they be before they have ended. The Church cannot analyze their authenticity until all the information from the first to the last apparition is brought before the panel. However, in the meantime, Pope John Paul II authorized the option to journey to Medjugorje to pray, confess, perform acts of penance, and fast.

Regardless of the Church's inability to make a determination, millions of pilgrims travel there each year. Medjugorje is one of the few places in the world where pilgrims actually are in the vicinity of a current apparition of Mary that is thought to be taking place. Pilgrims go there to hear the visionaries repeat Mary's messages, pray in the town church, climb Apparition Hill and Cross Mountain where the first apparitions occurred, and be near the Queen of Peace. Their hope is that Mary will take their prayers into her hands and help relieve them of their physical and mental anguish.

The majority of other busy Marian shrines are in honor of apparitions determined to be worthy of belief. As mentioned previously, the world's busiest Marian shrine is in Mexico City, Mexico. Nearly twenty million pilgrims venture to the Basilica of Our Lady of Guadalupe each year to honor Mary's apparitions to the peasant convert, Juan Diego, in 1531.

Relatively not far away is the site in Betania, Venezuela: the most recently approved apparition. There it is believed that a white-robed Mary first appeared to Maria Esperanza at her farm on March 25, 1976. The apparitions continued until Maria, and more than a hundred other people, saw Mary for the last time on March 25,

1984. Maria said Mary asked that people of all nations pray to God often.

In Akita, Japan, Sister Agnes Katsuko Sasagawa received messages from an angel beginning in 1969 and Mary in 1973. Sister Agnes suffered the wounds of the stigmata—the bleeding wounds associated with those Jesus suffered from the crucifixion—on her left hand. She also heard a voice from a wooden statue of Mary. Later, people witnessed the statue cry human tears, bleed human blood from the right hand, and sweat perfume. Pilgrims are welcomed to visit the chapel in the convent of the Handmaids of the Eucharist at Yuzawadai and see the statue. A Japanese-style Mary garden at the convent's entrance offers a peaceful place to pray.

From 1968 to 1971, in the city of Zeitoun near Cairo, Egypt, Mary appeared over the domes of Saint Mary's Coptic Church. Muslim laborers saw Mary first, followed by crowds exceeding two hundred and fifty thousand. They captured her image on television and personal cameras. Wearing a white robe and blue-white veil, Mary often was alone. Occasionally she held the infant Jesus and was accompanied by Saint Joseph. Witnesses also told stories of mysterious lights, fragrances from unknown sources, and white doves appearing from nowhere.

There are two Marian shrines in Belgium recognizing approved apparitions. Mary appeared eight times to eleven-year-old Mariette Becco in a family garden near

Banneux in 1933. Wearing a white gown with a blue sash and a white veil, Mary called herself the Virgin of the Poor. She promised to intercede for the needy, sick and suffering. She made a spring to flow in a ditch and told Mariette the water was for all nations to relieve the sick. A half-million pilgrims seek healing at the site of this apparition each year.

A million pilgrims visit the shrine in Beauraing, Belgium, annually where Mary appeared thirty-three times in a convent playground. Five children, aged nine to fifteen years of age, received these apparitions from 1932 to 1933. Mary announced she was the Immaculate Virgin, Mother of God, and Queen of Heaven. She asked the children to pray all the time.

The shrine at Fatima, Portugal honors Mary's messages to ten-year-old Lucia de Santos and her cousins, nine-year-old Francisco and seven-year-old Jacinta Marto. Mary, dressed in white, appeared six times between May and October 1917 in an area known as the Cova da Iria. Although quite plain, the sanctuary offers a dynamic spot for spiritual reflection. The open square leading to the basilica is reminiscent of a smaller version of St. Peter's Square in Vatican City.

During the daytime hours, Fatima pilgrims attend Mass or pray the rosary in various languages in the Basilica of Our Lady, Queen of the Holy Rosary, or in the Chapel of the Apparitions. The chapel is a clear, glass-sided structure erected on the exact site of the apparitions. It is not unusual to see people walking on their bloodied knees down a pathway to the chapel. At night, candlelight processions are held as priests and pilgrims sing *Ave, Ave, Ave, Maria,* following behind the Our Lady of Fatima statue. Pilgrims flock to the shrine year-round, but from May to October, hundreds of thousands pray there on the thirteenth of each month.

There are four significant Marian shrines in France. Our Lady of the Miraculous Medal is remembered in Rue du Back, Paris. Every year more than one million pilgrims visit the chapel in the motherhouse of the Congregation of the Daughters of Charity of Saint Vincent de Paul, where Mary appeared to a young novice named Catherine Laboure in 1830. Mary said she was the Immaculate Conception and asked for a medal to be made as she instructed.

Three-hundred and fifty-thousand people visit the shrine annually in Pont Main, France. In 1871 Mary appeared as a young woman dressed in a dark-blue dress with gold stars. She wore a black veil and gold crown. Ten-year-old Eugene and twelve-year-old Joseph Bernadette, Francoise Richer, and Jeanne-Marie Loose witnessed the apparitions. Mary told the group that Jesus is moved by compassion.

Each year one quarter of a million visitors go to the shrine at La Salute, France, that commemorates the apparition to eleven-year-old Maxim in Giraud and fourteen-year-old Melanie Calmat in 1846. Mary asked for conversion and penance. Pilgrims venturing to this site find a fragment of the stone where Mary sat weeping when the children saw her.

Perhaps the most famous of all Marian shrines is that of Lourdes. The site honors Mary's appearance to fourteen-year-old Bernadette Soubirous in 1858. Millions of pilgrims travel to Lourdes each year, many seeking miraculous healings. And many do indeed testify to receiving a miracle. Racks of canes and wheelchairs are left behind to testify to these claims.

The Catholic Church encourages devotion to, but has not officially approved, the apparitions of Our Lady of Knock, also known as Our Lady of Silence. One million visitors go to the shrine each year in memory of the August 21, 1879 apparition of Mary, St. Joseph and St. John the Evangelist to a small group of people. Also seen were a cross and a lamb on top of an altar. The apparition lasted for two hours at the door of a church in the country town of Knock, Ireland. Witnesses consisted of at least fifteen people between the ages of five and seventy-five years old.

Located in County Mayo, the Irish shrine is easily reached by train, bus or car. Lush greenery and floral gardens provide a peaceful, prayerful setting. Pilgrims walk these lovely grounds and attend the anointing of the sick, Stations of the Cross, perpetual adoration, and Masses in the basilica. They also touch a stone from the original church on which the apparition appeared.

꒰ ꒱

U.S. Shrines

In addition to these major Marian shrines, smaller ones
are scattered throughout the world. Each site features
a particular devotion. In the United States, there are
shrines to the Immaculate Heart of Mary, Our Lady of
Perpetual Help, *Neustra Senora de la Conquistador*, Our
Lady of the Angels, and others. Some of the sites de-
scribe a geographic area such as Our Lady of the Sierras,
Our Lady of the Highways, Our Lady of the Prairies, and
Mary, Queen of the Universe. There are multiple shrines
erected to the most popular Marian devotions such as
Our Lady of Guadalupe and Our Lady of Lourdes.

Perhaps the country's most unusual shrine is the
traveling statue known as Our Lady of the New Millennium. The structure, made from stainless-steel bands,
is thirty-three feet, eight inches in height and weighs
more than eight-thousand pounds. As an act of devotion to Our Lady, Carl Derma commissioned Charles
Cooper Parks to design and construct the sculpture in
1998. Blessed by Pope John Paul II during his visit to St.
Louis, Missouri, in 1999, the sculpture draws thousands
to pray. When Our Lady of the New Millennium arrives
in a town, local parishes sponsor events including prayer
services, processions and the recitation of the rosary.

Hundreds of thousands of pilgrims visit the Basilica
of the National Shrine of the Immaculate Conception in

Washington, D.C., which is the main Marian shrine and Catholic church in the United States. The massive structure of stone, brick, tile and mortar ranks among the ten largest churches in the world. It is dedicated to Mary, the Immaculate Conception, and patroness of the nation.

Visit and it won't be difficult to find a particular interest or place of comfort. The basilica is home to the largest collection of contemporary ecclesiastical art in the country and more than sixty-five chapels and oratories—places designated by the bishop for public or private worship. Each is spectacularly and uniquely decorated, illustrating the nation's extensive and diverse devotions to Mary. Some, such as the Bavarian oratory of Our Lady of Allotting, are exact replicas: gifts of solidarity from churches around the world.

⁂

Mary Gardens

If you don't want to, or cannot, travel beyond your own home, you can create your own shrine to Mary. This can be your private area where you pray and relax with our heavenly mother. You need not go to a distant land for Mary to hear your prayers or comfort you in your pain.

An altar can be created with a small table covered with a pretty cloth and an image of Mary. Place a chair nearby for you to sit and pray, or a small carpet on which to kneel. Add fresh or silk flowers or plants or create an entire garden for Mary.

Gardens are known to have been dedicated to Mary since the first centuries of Christianity. Monasteries constructed the earliest. As Marian devotion grew, so did the number of Mary gardens. During the Middle Ages, Mary's popularity was at its peak: Gardens were found in countless public and private areas.

An indoor or outdoor Mary garden may be constructed with a pot of specially-arranged plants, an arrangement of pots on a tabletop or patio, or a full-fledged garden. All you need are one or more plants and a statue, holy card or icon of Mary. Add an inviting pathway and a chair, bench or swing to create a comfortable, fragrant space to pray. The combination of religious articles and nature is tremendously soothing.

There are dozens of stories associating Mary with flowers and herbs (the sweet scent of roses and the purity of the white lily perhaps being the most common). It is said that the Angel Gabriel held a lily when the celestial being appeared before Mary to announce the conception of Jesus. When the Virgin consented, violets blossomed around her. Legend says that after Mary's passing from this world, Saint Thomas opened her tomb to prove that her body was assumed into heaven. He found the burial space filled with roses and lilies.

Other legends include the flower called "Our Lady's Shoes," which grew where Mary stepped on her way to see her cousin, Elizabeth. Lilies of the Valley are known as Mary's tears because when Mary cried at the cross her tears turned into this flower. In addition, many shrubs and herbs, such as lavender and rosemary, are associated with her because tradition says they only became fragrant after Mary laid her divine child's clothes across them to dry.

Flowers also are named for Mary's many attributes, physical characteristics, and experiences. The violet represents her modesty; the carnation, Mary's love of God. Snowdrop is the flower of purification. And the blue flag iris is known as Mary's Sword of Sorrow because of its deep purple-blue blossoms and sword-pointed leaves. Other flowers are named for the garments she wore, such as lady's buttons, lady's cloak, and lady's mantle.

The most common flower planted in a Mary garden is the rose. The word "rosary" originally meant "rose garden" or "garland of roses," correlating with the rosary being a garland or collection of prayers. The colors of the roses, and all flowers, are significant because of what they represent. Red roses are for sorrow, white for joy and purity, and yellow for Mary's glories. Early Christians called the marigold Mary's Gold. They placed these flowers around statues of Mary to symbolize the riches worthy of the Queen of Heaven and Earth. Other popular flowers include the forget-me-not, bachelor's button, Mary's Crown, zinnia, iris, and daffodil.

Herbs also may be planted in a Mary garden. Often included are basil, thyme, marjoram, spearmint and parsley. Their fragrance symbolizes Mary's sweetness.

❦ ❧

Your Sacred Space

Sacred spaces have the ability to tie a variety of devotions together and allow you to express your concerns on multiple levels. They offer a corner to contemplate, read the Bible or other devotional books, pray the rosary, listen to music, and display meaningful artwork. The shrine can be as simple or elaborate as you want, the goal being to create a space that promotes your prayer life and communication with Mary and Jesus.

This is most important during periods of grief recovery. Sacred space and quiet time are essential to healing. Many people try to stay busy and surround themselves with other people. However, these occasions need to balance with calm, quiet and prayerful reflection in a tranquil setting.

Your prayerful haven may be in or just outside of your own home or at a far-off pilgrimage destination. You may design and erect a Marian shrine or garden as a prayer request, in thanksgiving for an answered prayer, or as a show of devotion. Wherever this sacred space is, if you invite her, Mary will join you in prayer. When lonely, sad, angry or weary, ask our heavenly mother for help. She loves you dearly, and once you are aware of her love, you will find she is an incredible friend.

Chapter Six

Saint Mary-of-the-Woods, Sisters of Providence Mother-house, Providence Hall. Saint Mary-of-the-Woods, Indiana.

Devotion
in Our Mother's Arms

rief recovery is a period of healing unique to the grieving person. Everyone's experiences are different because there are so many variables involved. Recovery depends on the type of loss or hardship, the unique relationship you had with what or whom was lost, your physical, emotional and spiritual condition at the time of loss, how much preparation or advance notice you had, and an array of outside factors. The extent of family and faith community support also influences the healing process.

Psychologists identify various stages of grief that usually include denial, anger, bargaining, depression and acceptance. There also are a range of physical effects on the body such as lack of concentration, fatigue, shortness of breath, and overall feeling of illness. A loss of interest in things previously enjoyed, perhaps even the desire to pray and attend church, may result. The stages don't typically follow a set pattern but rather fluctuate and overlap for various periods of time. Grief may appear to end but then return again when you least expect it.

However you grieve, know that grieving is a normal, human response. The period of bereavement runs its own course at its own rate. To lose what is dear to you is painful. You may wish to ignore or suppress the mourning. Yet experiencing the pain is necessary, for if it's ignored or rushed, it only will resurface later.

Initially, there often is a sense of numbness. The lack of feeling can be frightening. Allow yourself to grieve. Don't fight it but rather find comfort in it. And pray for help. Through prayer your pain evolves into peace, your loss into a celebration of someone's life or the joyful experiences you once enjoyed.

If you trust in Jesus, you will have peace in this life and the next. This is Jesus' promise to us. Throughout the Gospel we hear Jesus telling us not to let our problems get the best of us (see John 14:1, 27). Jesus promised that he answers all of our prayers. He said, "All things can be done for the one who believes" (Mark 8:23). He also said that anything we ask for in his name will be granted (see John 14:14).

Remembering these promises is especially challenging in times of sorrow. However, if you believe in Jesus, you must trust what he says is true. From the condition of your life it may appear he doesn't hear you, but have faith that Jesus does. He will answer you in the way he knows is best. Do not lose hope. Recovery will come with time, rest, nourishment, diversion, support, hope and prayer.

And if you ask, Mary will help you heal. She loves you because you are a child of God and a brother or sister in Christ. You are her child. Her arms are open and waiting. Send her your love and your prayers. You only need to call on her and she will answer you.

There are so many ways in which to pray. Show your devotion using the method that is most meaningful to you. Whether it is with fine art, music, words, movement, or sacred space, utilize your God-given talents and knowledge. Mary responds no matter how you pray. She prays with you and comforts you while you recover. She fills the empty spaces in your heart and warms them with love for Jesus and her love for you.

Do not hesitate to go to her in prayer. Do not waste another moment suffering alone. Your heavenly mother is waiting for you. As Mary promised Saint Juan Diego, she protects you in the folds of her mantle, in the crossing of her loving arms.

Appendix

Feasts of the Blessed Virgin Mary

Mary is honored on several days throughout the year. These dates recognize her in biblical, dogmatic (Church doctrine), or regional references. Following are the feast days commonly celebrated in the Christian, particularly the Roman Catholic and the Orthodox, Church.

January 1: Solemnity of Mary the Mother of God

On this day Mary is honored as the *Theotokos*, the God-Bearer, the Mother of God. This is a day of Holy Obligation in the Catholic Church, meaning that attendance at Mass is required.

February 2: Presentation of Our Lord

This feast day recognizes the presentation of Jesus in the temple by Mary and Joseph according to the Gospel of Luke.

February 11: Feast of Our Lady of Lourdes

Mary's apparitions to Bernadette Soubirous in 1858 and the hope of the disabled and infirmed who continue to seek healings on behalf of Our Lady of Lourdes are remembered on this day.

March 19: St. Joseph, Husband of Mary

March 25: Solemnity of the Annunciation of the Lord

The feast of the Annunciation most likely dates to the Council of Ephesus in 431 and celebrates the Angel Gabriel's announcement to Mary on behalf of the Lord that she would bear the Son of God.

May 31: Feast of the Visitation of the Blessed Virgin Mary to Elizabeth

When Mary visited her cousin, Elizabeth, the unborn John the Baptist leapt for joy within Elizabeth's womb. Elizabeth said to Mary, "Blessed is the fruit of your womb, Jesus."

Saturday after Second Sunday after Pentecost: Immaculate Heart of Mary

Mary's pure and holy heart is filled with love for all of us and especially for her son, Jesus.

July 16: Memorial of Our Lady of Mount Carmel

Mary is remembered on this day for appearing to St. Simon Stock in the year 1251 and presenting him with the Brown Scapular.

August 15: Solemnity of the Assumption of the Blessed Virgin Mary

The Assumption is a day of Holy Obligation. Most likely, the feast was first celebrated in the fifth or sixth century. It commemorates Mary being assumed into heaven, body and soul. Pope Pius XII declared this belief as official Church doctrine in 1950.

August 22: Memorial of the Queenship of Mary

Our Lady is honored on this day as queen of heaven and earth.

September 8: Feast of the Birth of the Blessed Virgin Mary

Mary's birth is celebrated on September 8. This feast is believed to have originated in Syria or Palestine at the beginning of the sixth century and was recognized by the Roman church by the end of the seventh.

September 15: Feast of Our Lady of Sorrows

Mary encountered several sorrowful events in her life on earth. These sorrows include Simeon's Prophecy, the flight into Egypt, the loss of Jesus in the Temple, her meeting with Jesus on his way to Calvary, Jesus' crucifixion, Mary's receiving the dead body of Jesus, and Jesus' burial.

October 7: Memorial of Our Lady of the Rosary

The feast of Our Lady of the Rosary honors Mary for offering us the rosary to aid with meditating upon the mysteries of Jesus' incarnation, life, death, resurrection and ascension. Mary told the visionaries at Fatima that she is the Lady of the Rosary.

November 21: Memorial of the Presentation of the Blessed Virgin Mary

Legend has it that when Mary was three years old her parents, Anne and Joachim, brought her to the temple and dedicated her to God. We honor Mary on this day for life-long devotion to God.

December 8: Solemnity of the Immaculate Conception

From as early as the seventh century it has been believed that Mary was conceived without sin. Pope Pius IX proclaimed her Immaculate Conception as a dogma of faith in 1854.

December 12: Feast of Our Lady of Guadalupe

This feast day is celebrated particularly in Mexico in memory of Mary's appearance to Juan Diego.

Marian Hymns

Hail, Holy Queen Enthroned Above

Hail, holy Queen enthroned above, O Maria.
Hail, Queen of mercy and of love, O Maria.

Triumph, all ye cherubim, Sing with us, ye seraphim,
Heaven and earth resound the hymn:
Salve, salve, salve Regina!

Our life, our sweetness, here below, O Maria!
Our hope in sorrow and in woe, O Maria!

Triumph, all ye cherubim, Sing with us, ye seraphim,
Heaven and earth resound the hymn:
Salve, salve, salve Regina!

Immaculate Mary

Immaculate Mary, your praises we sing;
You reign now in splendor with Jesus our King.
Ave, ave, ave, Maria! Ave, ave, Maria!
In heaven, the blessed your glory proclaim;
On earth we, your children, invoke your sweet name.
Ave, ave, ave, Maria! Ave, ave, Maria!
We pray for the Church, our true Mother on earth,
And beg you to watch o'er the land of our birth.
Ave, ave, ave, Maria! Ave, ave, Maria!

Lovely Lady

Lovely Lady dressed in blue—
Teach me how to pray.
God was just your little boy,
Tell me what to say,
Did you lift him up, sometimes,
Gently on your knee?
Did you sing to him the way,
Mother does to me?
Did you hold his hand at night?
Did you ever try
Telling stories of the world?
Oh! And did he cry?
Do you really think he cares
If I tell him things—
Little things that happen? And
Do the angels' wings
Make a noise? And can he hear
Me if I speak low?
Does he understand me now?
Lovely Lady dressed in blue—
Teach me how to pray.
God was just your little boy,
And you know the way.

Mother Dearest, Mother Fairest

Mother dearest, Mother fairest,
Help of all who call on thee,
Virgin purest, brightest, rarest,
Help us help, we cry to thee.
Mary, help us, help we pray,
Mary, help us, help we pray,
Help us in all care and sorrow:
Mary, help us, help we pray.
Lady, help in pain and sorrow,
Soothe those rack'd on beds of pain,
May the golden light of morrow,
Bring them health and joy again.
Help our priests, our virgins holy,
Help our pope, long may he reign.
Pray that we who sing thy praises,
May in heav'n all meet again.
Lady, help the wounded soldier,
Set the pining captive free,
Help the sailor in mid-ocean,
Help those in their agony.
Lady, help the absent loved ones,
How we miss their presence here,
May the hand of thy protection
Guide and guard them far and near.

On This Day, O Beautiful Mother

On this day, O beautiful Mother;
On this day we give thee our love,
Near thee, Madonna, fondly we hover,
Trusting thy gentle care to prove.
On this day we ask to share,
Dearest Mother, thy sweet care;
Aid us ere our feet astray
Wander from thy guiding way.
Queen of Angels, deign to hear, thy dear
Children's humble prayer.
Young hearts gain, O Virgin pure, sweetly
To thyself allure.

Prayers to Mary

Angelus

V: The angel of the Lord declared unto Mary.

R: And she conceived of the Holy Spirit.

Hail Mary full of grace, the Lord is with you. Blessed are you among women, and blessed is the fruit of your womb, Jesus. Holy Mary, Mother of God, pray for us sinners now and at the hour of our death. Amen.

V: Behold the handmaid of the Lord.

R: Be it done unto me according to your word.

Hail Mary . . .

V: And the Word was made flesh.

R: And dwelt among us.

Hail Mary . . .

V: Pray for us, O holy Mother of God.

R: That we may be made worthy of the promises of Christ.

Let us pray: Pour forth, we beseech you, O Lord, your grace into our hearts, that we, to whom the incarnation of Christ your son was made known by the message of an angel, may by his passion and cross be brought to the glory of his resurrection; through the same Christ our Lord. Amen.

Consecration to the Immaculate Heart of Mary

Virgin Mary, Mother of God and our mother, to your immaculate heart we consecrate ourselves in an act of total entrustment to the Lord. By you we will be led to Christ. By him, and with him, we will be led to the Father. We will walk in the light of faith, and we will do everything so that the world may believe that Jesus Christ is the one sent by the Father. With him we wish to carry his love and salvation to the ends of the earth. Under the protection of your immaculate heart, we will be one people with Christ. We will be witnesses of his resurrection. By him we will be led to the Father, for the glory of the Most Holy Trinity, whom we adore, praise and bless forever. Amen.

Hail, Holy Queen

Hail, Holy Queen, Mother of Mercy; our life, our sweetness and our hope. To you do we cry, poor banished children of Eve. To you do we send up our sighs, mourning and weeping in this valley of tears. Turn then, O most gracious advocate, your eyes of mercy toward us, and after this our exile, show unto us the blessed fruit of your womb, Jesus. O clement, O loving, O sweet Virgin Mary.

V: Pray for us, O holy Mother of God.

R: That we may become worthy of the promises of Christ.

Immaculate Mother of Jesus

Immaculate Mother of Jesus, we honor you as God's chosen one, beautiful, beloved, and free from all sin. Keep watch over us, pray that we rise above our sins and failings and come to share the fullness of grace. Be a mother to us in the order of grace by assisting us to live your obedience, your faith, your hope and your love. Amen.

Memorare

Remember, O most gracious Virgin Mary, that never was it known that anyone who fled to your protection, implored your help, or sought your intercession was left unaided. Inspired with this confidence, I fly unto you, O Virgin of virgins, my Mother. To you I come; before you I stand, sinful and sorrowful. O Mother of the World Incarnate, despise not my petitions, but in your mercy hear and answer me.
Amen.

Prayer to the Blessed Virgin

O Most beautiful flower of Mount Carmel, fruitful vine, splendor of Heaven, Blessed Mother of the Son of God, Immaculate Virgin, assist me in this my necessity. O Star of the Sea, help me and show me herein you are my mother.

O Holy Mary, Mother of God, Queen of Heaven and

Earth, I humbly beseech you from the bottom of my heart, to help me in this necessity; there are none that can withstand your power.

O, show me herein you are my mother. O Mary, conceived without sin, pray for us who have recourse to you. *Repeat three times.*

Sweet Mother, I place this cause in your hands. *Repeat three times.*
Amen.

Novena to Our Lady of Perpetual Help

Mother of Perpetual Help, numerous clients continually surround your holy picture all imploring your mercy. All bless you as the assured help of the miserable, all feel the benefit of your motherly protection. With confidence, then, do we present ourselves before you in our misery. See, dear Mother, the many evils to which we are exposed; see how numerous are our wants. Trials and sorrows often depress us; reverses of fortune and privations often grievous bring misery into our lives; everywhere we meet the cross. Have pity, Compassionate Mother, on us and our dear ones; especially in this our necessity (*state your request here*). Help us, dear Mother, in our distress; deliver us from all our ills; or, if it be the will of God that we should suffer still longer, grant that we may

endure all with love and patience. These graces we expect of you with confidence, because you are our perpetual help. Amen.
Say three or five Hail Marys.

Novena to Our Lady of the Miraculous Medal
Pray the following prayers daily for nine days.

Come Holy Spirit, fill the hearts of your faithful and kindle in them the fire of your love. Send forth your spirit, and they shall be created.

And you shall renew the face of the earth.

Let us pray. O God, who has instructed the hearts of the faithful by the light of the Holy Spirit, grant us in the name Spirit to be truly wise and ever to rejoice in his consolation. Through Jesus Christ our Lord.

Amen.

O Mary, conceived without sin,
Pray for us who have recourse to you.
Repeat three times.

Lord Jesus Christ, who has glorified your mother, the blessed Virgin Mary, immaculate from the first moment of her conception, grant that all who devoutly implore her protection on earth may eternally enjoy your presence in heaven. Lord Jesus Christ, who for the accomplishment of your greatest works has chosen the weak things of the world, that no flesh may glory in your sight, and who for a better and more widely diffused belief in the Immaculate Conception of your mother, has wished that the Miraculous Medal be manifested to Saint Catherine Laboure, grant we ask you that, filled with like humility, we may glorify this mystery by word and work.

Amen.

Glossary

Annunciation: The announcement by the angel Gabriel to Mary that she would conceive a son, the Messiah.

Apparition: Vision of Jesus, Mary, an angel, or saint.

Bible: The collection of books written by human authors but believed inspired by the Holy Spirit.

Commandment: Requirements for true worship and morality in order to attain full union with God.

Conversion: The turning away from sin and turning toward God.

Divine: Relating to God.

Dogma: A teaching of the Church that the faithful are obliged to obey.

End of Times: End of the world as we know it. The final reality of the planet, the day of Last Judgment and the second coming of Jesus Christ.

Holy Father: The father of the Christian faith, the pope.

Incarnation: The union of the divine nature of the Second Person of the Trinity with the human nature of Jesus in order to accomplish the work of our redemption.

Immaculate Conception: Doctrine that Mary was born without the stain of Original Sin.

Imposition of Hands: Ancient symbol of blessing or consecration.

Intercession: Prayers made to God on behalf of others, whether living or deceased.

Koran: Holy book of the religion of Islam.

Labyrinth: A patterned pathway, often in a circular pattern, used for mediation and prayer. Unlike a maze, the path is continuous with no choices, dead-ends, or obstacles.

Mediatrix: The doctrine that Christ's graces flow through Mary.

Messiah: God's anointed one.

Miracle: An unexplained occurrence that glorifies God.

Reconciliation: The effect of Christ's saving passion, death and resurrection. A term used for the Sacrament of Penance.

Sacramentals: Specific objects and activities instituted by the Church to increase devotion and to deflect evil.

Scapular: Sacramental consisting of two swatches of cloth connected by two long cords to be worn with one cloth in front and one in back. A symbolic version of a garment worn as part of a religious habit.

Sin: The deliberate action of turning away from God and Divine Law

Veneration: Devotion to saints and other holy people.

Virginity: The state of lifelong abstinence from sexual intercourse.

Visionary: One who sees something that is naturally invisible.

Labyrinth Design

Marian Religious and Lay Organizations

A wide range of Marian lay and religious organizations promote prayer and devotion to Jesus through Mary. Some groups are quite small. Others are internationally strong. Most disperse literature and prayers in her honor. These organizations serve as a basic devotional presence and encourage attendance at daily mass, prayer—especially with the rosary—and frequent confession. Several of these groups also require a limited to total commitment of service.

Following are some of these organizations and their addresses. Please contact them or visit their website for further information. For a more complete list, see the University of Dayton's online directory, Pastoral Marian Organizations in the United States: www.udayton.edu/mary/pastoral.html

Association of Marian Helpers
Eden Hill
Stockbridge, MA 01263
Phone: 1-413-298-3691
www.marian.org/association

The Association of the Miraculous Medal
1811 West St. Joseph St.
Perryville, MO 63775
www.amm.org

The Blue Army
World Apostate of Fatima
Blue Army Shrine
PO Box 976
Washington NJ 07882
www.bluearmy.com

The Cenacle of Our Lady of Divine Providence
702 Bayview Ave.
Clearwater, FL 33759-4251
www.divineprovidence.org/Cenacle.htm

Legion of Mary
PO Box 1313
St. Louis, MO 63188
www.legion-of-mary.ie

Marist Laity in the United States
www.maristlaity.com/index.html

Militia of the Immaculata National Center
1600 W. Park Ave.
Libertyville, IL 60048
Phone: 1-847-367-7800, ext. 246
www.consecration.com

Missionary Oblates of Mary Immaculate Lay Associations
Sr. Geri Furmanek, ASC
Oblate Associates
224 South De Mazenod Drive
Belleville, IL 62223-1035
www.omiusa.org/OMIassociatesforms.htm

Our Lady of Mercy Lay Carmelites
Governo House
Holy Spirit Church
Fremont, CA
www.olmlaycarmelites.org

Queen of All Hearts
26 South Saxon Ave.
Bay Shore, NY 11706-8993
www.memorare.com/mary/queenh.html

Queen of the Americas Guild
PO Box 851
St. Charles, IL 60174
1-630-585-1822
www.queenoftheamericasguild.org

Sisters of Mary, Mother of the Eucharist
4597 Warren Road
Ann Arbor, MI 48105
www.sistersofmary.org

Bibilography

Articles

Aviva, Elyn. "Walking the labyrinth. A Journey on a Sacred Path." *The Quest*, Summer 1998.

"Marian Apparitions of the 20th Century." *The Mary Page.* http://www.udayton.edu/mary/resources/aprtable.html.

McMahon, Colin. "Denied asylum by U.S., sailor turned to God," *Chicago Tribune*. July 1, 2001.

Roten, Rev. Hohann G. "Evangelization with Mary." *The Mary Page: Meditations* http://www.udayton.edu/mary/meditations/evangelizaton.html.

Wooden, Cindy. "Scapular Comeback? Carmelite hopes anniversary renews popularity," *The Observer*. March 16, 2001.

Booklets and Pamphlets

Attach Great Importance to Your Scapular. NY: The International Fatima Rosary Crusade Fatima Center, 1941.

Cadhain, Siobhan C. Bean Ui. "The Vision in Marble." Ireland: Knock Shrine Society.

Carter, S.J., Fr. Edward. *The Spirituality of Fatima and Medjugorje.* Morrow, Ohio: Shepherds of Christ Publications, 1994.

Deery, Reverend Lawrence A., Imprimatur, Most Reverend Timothy J. Harrington, Bishop of Worcester. *Garment of Grace*. Buffalo, NY: The Immaculate Heart Publications, 9 March 1990.

Glavich, S.N.D., Mary Kathleen. *Handbook for Catholics*. Chicago, IL: Loyola Press, 1995.

Grady, Bishop Thomas J. *Mary First Disciple. Reflections on Mary of Nazareth*. Boston, MA: Pauline Books and Media, 1992.

Korn, C.Ss.R., Brother Daniel (Compiled by). *Marian Prayers and Devotions*. Liguori, MO: Liguori, 2000.

Lovaski, SVD, Father. *Mary My Mother*. New York, NY: Catholic Book Publishing Co., 1978.

Marian Chapel Prayers. Washington, D.C.: Basilica of the National Shrine of the Immaculate Conception.

Marian Prayers. Newburgh, NY: Dominican Sisters of Hope.

Outlines of the Catholic Faith. St. Paul, MN: The Leaflet Missal Company.

Pocket Book of Prayers for All Occasions. Washington, D.C.: Basilica of the National Shrine of the Immaculate Conception.

Spirituality and Healing in Medicine, 20-22 March 1999, (Brochure).

Books and References

The Academy of the Immaculate. *A Handbook on Guadalupe*. New Bedford, MA: Our Lady's Chapel, 1997.

Artress, Dr. Lauren, *Walking a Sacred Path. Rediscovering the Labyrinth as a Spiritual Tool,* New York, NY: Riverhead Books, 1995.

Ball, Ann. *A Handbook of Catholic Sacramentals*. Huntington, Indiana: Our Sunday Visitor, Inc., 1991.

Balthasar, Hans Urs von and Joseph Cardinal Ratzinger. *Mary. The Church at the Source*. San Francisco: Ignatius Press, 1997.

Begg, Ean. *The Cult of the Black Virgin*. New York: Arkana, 1985.

Bernardin, Joseph Cardinal. *The Gift of Peace*. NY: Image Books Doubleday, 1998.

Boyer, Marie-France. *The Cult of the Virgin*. London: Thames & Hudson Ltd, 2000.

Brown, Raphael (Compiled by). *The Life of Mary as Seen by the Mystics*. Rockford, IL: Tan Books and Publishers, Inc., 1951.

Brown, Raymond E. and Karl P. Donfried, Joseph A. Fitzmyer, John Reumann, eds. *Mary in the New Testament*. Philadelphia: Fortress Press, 1978 and New York: Paulist Press, 1978.

Catholic Encyclopedia on CD-ROM

Compton's Interactive Encyclopedia. Compton's New-Media, Inc., 1994, 1995.

Deits, Bob. *Life After Loss: A Personal Guide dealing with Death, Divorce, Job Change and Relocation.* Tucson: Fisher Books, 1988.

Donofrio, Beverly. *Looking for Mary: or, the Blessed Mother and Me.* New York, NY: Penguin Compass, 2000.

Fatima in Lucia's Own Words. Sister Lucia's Memoirs. Still River, MA: The Ravengate Press, 1998.

Glavich, Mary Kathleen. *The Catholic Companion to Mary.* Skokie, IL: ACTA Publications, 2007.

The Glories of Czestochowa and Jasna Gora. Worcester, Massachusetts: Our Lady of Czestochowa Foundation, 1981.

Groeschel, C.F.R., Fr. Benedict J. *A Still, Small Voice. A Practical Guide on Reported Revelations.* San Francisco, CA: Ignatius Press, 1993.

Hahn, Scott. Hail, Holy Queen. *The Mother of God in the Word of God.* New York, NY: Doubleday, 2001.

Hiesberger, Jean Marie, General Editor. *The Catholic Bible. Personal Study Edition.* New York: Oxford University Press, 1995.

Hickman, Martha Whitmore. *Healing After Loss.* New York: Avon Books, 1994.

Hoever, S.O.Cist, Ph.D., Rev. Hugo H. Editor. *Saint Joseph Daily Missal.* New York: Catholic Book Publishing Co., 1959.

Holy Apostles Convent. *The Life of the Virgin Mary, the Theotokos.* Buena Vista: Holy Apostles Convent and

Dormition Skete, 1989.

The Holy Bible. New Revised Standard Version, Catholic Edition. Oxford, NY: Oxford University Press, 1999.

Huels, J.C.D., John M. *The Pastoral Companion.* Quincy, IL: Franciscan Press. Quincy University, 1995.

International Commission on English in the Liturgy. *Shorter Book of Blessings.* New York, NY: Catholic Book Publishing Co, 1990.

James, John W. & Frank Cherry. *The Grief Recovery Handbook. A Step-by-Step Program for Moving Beyond Loss.* New York: Harper & Row, 1988.

Johnson, Ph.D., Kevin Orlin. *Why do Catholics Do That? A Guide to the Teachings and Practices of the Catholic Church.* New York: Ballantine Books, 1994.

Johnston, Francis. *Fatima: The Great Sign.* Rockford, IL: Tan Books and Publishers, Inc., 1980

Katz, Melissa R. and Robert A. Orsi. *Divine Mirrors.* Oxford: University Press, 2001

Kornfield, Margaret Zipse. *Cultivating Wholeness. A Guide to Care and Counseling in Faith Communities.* New York: The Continuum International Publishing Group Inc, 2003.

Krymow, Vincenzina. *Mary's Flowers. Gardens, Legends & Meditations.* Cincinnati: St. Anthony Messenger Press, 1989.

Kubler-Ross, Elisabeth and David Kessler. *Life Lessons.* New York: Touchstone, 2002.

Kubler-Ross, Elisabeth. *On Death and Dying.* New

York: Macmillan Publishing Co., Inc, 1969.

Kushner, Harold. *Who Needs God.* New York: Pocket Books, 1989.

Libreria Editrice Vaticana, Citta del Vaticano. *Catechism of the Catholic Church.* Dubuque, IA: Brown-Roa, 1994.

"Mary, the Mother of Jesus," *The Columbia Encyclopedia Online,* Sixth Edition, 2001.

Monumenti, Musei e Gallerie Pontificie. *The Mother of God: Art Celebrates Mary.* Vatican Museums and the Pope John Paul II Cultural Center, 2001.

Panati, Charles. *Sacred Origins of Profound Things.* New York, NY: Penguin Group, 1996.

Pelikan, Jaroslav. *Mary Through the Centuries. Her Place in the History of Cultures.* New Haven and London: Yale University, 1996.

Quenot, Michael. *The Icon.* Crestwood, NY: St. Vladimir's Seminary Press, 1996.

Redmont, Jane. *When in Doubt, Sing. Prayer in Daily Life.* New York, New York: Harper Collins, 1999.

Ross, Floyd H. and Tynette Hills. *The Great Religions by Which Men Live.* Greenwich, Conn: Facett Premier 1956.

Ruugles, Ph.D, Robin. *Apparition Shrines. Places of Pilgrimage amd Prayer.* Boston: Daughters of St. Paul, 2000.

Sanders, M. Catherine. *Grief: The Mourning After. Dealing with Adult Bereavement.* New York: John Wiley & Sons, 1989.

Smith, Huston. *The Illustrated World's Religions. A Guide to Our Wisdom Traditions.* New York, NY: HarperSanFrancisco, 1991.

Smith, Huston. *Why Religion Matters. The Fate of the Human Spirit in an Age of Disbelief.* New York, NY: HarperSanFrancisco, 2001.

Straudacher, Carol. *A Time to Grieve: Meditations for healing after the death of a loved one.* New York: Harpercollins Publishers, 1994.

Stravinskas, Peter M. J., Ph.D., S.T.D. *Catholic Dictionary.* Huntington, IN: Our Sunday Visitor, Inc., 2002.

Walsh, William Thomas. *Our Lady of Fatima.* New York, New York: Doubleday, 1954.

Weible, Wayne. *The Final Harvest. Medjugorje at the End of the Century.* Brewster, MA: Paraclete Press, 1999.

Wicks,Robert J. *Clinical Handbook of Pastoral Counseling* Volume 1. New York: Paulist Press, 1993.

Wicks, Robert J. *Handbook of Spirituality for Ministers.* Volume 1.New York, Paulist Press, 1995.

Wuthnow, Robert. *Christianity in the 21st Century. Reflections on the Challenges Ahead.* New York: Oxford University Press, 1993.

Videos

Lourdes. Pilgrimage & Healing, Worcester PA: Vision Video.

Acknowledgments

A book never comes from the author alone. Knowledge is gathered from a multitude of sources. Many of these sources are books, but people also offer information, guidance, direction and insight.

I am very grateful to the people who shared their time and knowledge. God's greatest blessings to me are in the loving family and friends by which I'm surrounded. I am most thankful for the awesome gift of a loving husband, children, step-children, sisters, brothers, in-laws, nieces, nephews, aunts, uncles, cousins and many friends.

My sister, Patricia Doyle Brewer, and cousin, Carol Glab, were the first to read through rough manuscripts. I thank them for their time and suggestions. My daughter, Erin Cannella, took the time to read a later manuscript, which I also appreciate.

I wish to acknowledge my friend, Dr. Susan Holstein, clinical psychologist, for the many resources she shared with me and her expert guidance on grief recovery. Terry Urban, a fellow student at St. Mary-of-the-Woods, Indiana, generously loaned me a trunk-load of books on icons and religious art. I thank her very much.

In addition, I always appreciate those whom I consider mentors including the Reverend Monsignor Joseph Jarmoluk from my parish, St. Peter Church, Geneva, Illinois, and Sister Alexa Suelzer, The Reverend Bernard

LaMontagne, and Dr. Virginia Unverzagt, all from St. Mary-of-the-Woods, Indiana. I'm also appreciative of all the Sisters of Providence and Rev. Bruce Ludeke (Parochial Vicar), also from St. Peter.

My thanks to those who helped me with first-hand cultural celebrations of Mary, including Jackie and Gabriel Fuentes and Teodora Arredondo for information on Spanish culture and devotion; the Reverend Akan Simon for information on African devotion; and Nijole Kasuba, for telling me about Lithuanian devotion.

Thank you also to my contract advisor, John Gile from the National Writers Union for the many volunteer hours he spent assisting me. I also am grateful for all of the ACTA Publications family. I appreciate working with publisher Greg Pierce, editor L.C. Fiore, and the rest of the publishing team.